NATURAL NURSERY KNITS

Twenty handknit projects for the new baby

ERIKA KNIGHT

photography by Kristin Perers

Quadrille
PUBLISHING

Introduction 8
NATURAL NURSERY COLLECTION 12

NATURAL NURSERY PATTERNS 76
· Cellular blanket 78 · Teddy bear 80 · Initialled
washcloth 84 · Classic cardigan 88 · Hare doorstop 90
· Scented cushion 94 · Rabbit rattle 96 · Hat and
boots 98 · Fairisle papoose 100 · First blanket 102
· Dress and pants 104 · Recycled rag basket 108 ·
Sweater and trousers 110 · Bootees and bonnet 114
· Lace cushion 118 · Bird mobile 120 · Soaker
pants 122 · Heirloom cot cover 124 · Spotty
giraffe 128 · Nightie and hat 130

Templates 134 · Recommended yarns 138 ·
Pattern instructions 139 · Garment care 140 ·
Acknowledgements 142

INTRODUCTION

This book always promised to be a pleasure to write. Bringing together two of my passions – knitting for tiny babies and natural yarns – what better occasion is there to go eco friendly than at the beginning of a new life? We all want to make what we believe to be the best choices for our children's wellbeing, so when it comes to choosing yarns for knitting for your baby, select authentic natural fibres whenever possible.

Nothing evokes fond memories of childhood so vividly as a pair of tiny baby bootees, a quintessential teddy bear or a cosy first blanket. This collection of nostalgic nursery knits is designed to welcome a newborn into the world – from dainty baby shoes and an adorably simple layette to luxuriously soft throws, pillows and characterful soft toys that are destined to become toybox favourites.

Made from beautiful, natural and sustainable yarns and trims, all of the projects are knitted in simple stitches and incorporate small design details that make a practical difference, like the integral scratch mittens on the nightie (see pages 72–3 and 130–132).

Of course, once baby has outgrown the knitwear, it can be washed, pressed and put away for your next baby or passed on to a relative, friend or neighbour. As generations have done before with their baby clothes, this is just simple, natural recycling. It's very reassuring to know that what you knit is not only kind to baby but is also gentle on the earth. Lovingly knitted, each piece you make is sure to become a keepsake of the future.

NATURAL YARNS

Derived from either animal or plant sources, natural yarns tend to have unique properties that give each project a particular character. I prefer to use baby animal fibres, such as alpaca and cashmere, for their natural softness and inherent luxury. However, other favourites include organic plant fibres, such as cotton and hemp, that are free from pesticides and chemical fertilisers. All these natural yarns absorb moisture and allow the skin to breathe, whilst remaining soft and comfortable to wear. When one invests time, dedication and love into every stitch in excited anticipation of an impending new life, using natural yarns is so worthwhile.

BABY ALPACA

A luxurious fibre to rival cashmere (but actually with less of a propensity to pill). With a beautiful drape, subtle sheen and extreme softness, it glides through the fingers and so is great for hand knitting. Due to its hollow fibres and microscopic air pockets, pure alpaca is completely thermal. It retains warmth whilst being breathable and absorbs moisture, making it an ideal choice for baby blankets and cardigans.

Alpaca comes in a large number of natural shades, from white through beiges and greys to rich browns. A truly noble natural yarn.

BAMBOO

Bamboo yarn is derived from a grass that is harvested and distilled into cellulose, which is then spun into a yarn. A renewable and sustainable resource, bamboo thrives with no need for any pesticides or artificial fertilisers, it is harvested without killing the plant, and it only is a few months before it is ready to be harvested again. All this makes bamboo a very eco-friendly yarn. Pure bamboo fibre is biodegradable and naturally antibacterial. It is cool to wear, taking moisture away from the skin and allowing it to breathe. Bamboo yarn has a wonderful drape and natural sheen; next to your skin, it feels similar to silk and so it is a perfect choice when knitting baby's welcome blanket. Garments made from bamboo are luxuriously soft, smooth and comfortable.

COTTON

Cotton grown organically is a natural vegetable fibre free from pesticides and artificial fertilisers, and one that is approved by a recognised regulating and certifying body. The organic cotton I prefer to use is fully certified; traceable all the way from seed to yarn store. Furthermore, the farmers are paid a living wage for its cultivation. Organic cotton is of a higher quality than conventional cotton; longer fibres result in softer but more durable and absorbent fabric. For a baby's delicate, sensitive skin, when the gentlest natural material is called for, organic cotton is the perfect choice.

MILK COTTON

Milk cotton is an extraordinarily soft yarn, which is so-called because it contains 30% milk protein. To produce the yarn, milk is dehydrated and skimmed, after which the milk protein casein is extracted. Once the protein is fluidised, it can then be spun and blended with other fibres, such as cotton. The result is an extremely smooth and fluid yarn that drapes and takes colour well, a lovely yarn for nursery projects, especially tiny shoes and bonnets.

HEMP

A perfect yarn for handknitting: 100% natural with a dry handle, subtle sheen and natural drape. Cool in summer, repelling 90% of UVA rays, and warm in winter, the wearer is kept comfortable at all times. Hemp is a robust fibre that gets softer each time it is washed. Hemp is the world's leading renewable resource; it can grow in virtually any soil and climate. It is excellent for reclaiming otherwise unusable land and as it is unpalatable to insects, it requires no pesticides. Knitting with hemp requires a little adjustment and slightly more time. Like linen, hemp has no natural elasticity, so once knitted, traditional methods of blocking and steaming enhance the appearance and softness of the finished fabric and create a truly timeless piece.

PLANT AND HERB DYES

Colour is an enormously important factor to consider when selecting natural yarns for babies. The naturally occurring colours of fibres can be very beautiful, especially those of baby alpaca and rare sheeps breed wools. Naturally marled, such yarns vary from ecru through soft grey to vicuna brown. With a yarn like alpaca you can be reassured that no bleach, chemicals or mordents have been used, which might irritate baby's skin or exacerbate any allergies. Elsewhere I have chosen organic cottons that are naturally dyed using plants and herbs, which produce no toxicity, just subtle pretty colours.

Organically grown cotton yarn is coloured with sustainable natural dyes. Likewise, the dyeing process is sustainable and harms neither the environment nor the people who depend upon it. Only natural plant and herb dyes are used, which produce no toxic effluent and to keep them chemical-free there are no mordents. Instead, the natural dye stuffs are fixed on to the fibre by the addition of salt alone. Due to their organic nature, you will find there is some colour variation in each shade, but this simply adds to the yarn's unique beauty.

To ensure the longevity of any naturally dyed yarn, avoid prolonged exposure to direct sunlight and follow the recommended garment care instructions. These natural variations do not in any way affect the quality or efficiency of the product.

ANNATTO (LIPSTICK TREE)

A red dye from the pulp of a fruit indigenous to the Caribbean and Central and South America. It is also used for colouring dairy products and confectionery and was once used to treat fevers and kidney disease.

LOGWOOD

A chipped and fermented wood grown in tropical America, which is used in violet, blue, grey and black dyes. A mild astringent, it is also used in treating chronic dysentery.

MADDER

A prickly herb from southern Europe grown as animal fodder, but whose roots can be powdered and used to produce many shades of red, pink, lilac, purple, brown, orange and black. It is reputed to ease cases of jaundice.

BRAZILWOOD

A New World heartwood that revolutionised the world of sixteenth-century fashion with a true red dye the colour of burning coals ('brieze') and gave birth to a nation.

YELLOWWOOD/CUBAWOOD

Trees with a yellow heart wood, used for dyeing browns, black and yellows. The bark can be used in a gargle for sore throats.

QUEBRACHO

Tall evergreen tree from South America with particularly dense 'axebreaker' wood that is a natural source of tannin. Can be used to help in cases of asthma and emphysema.

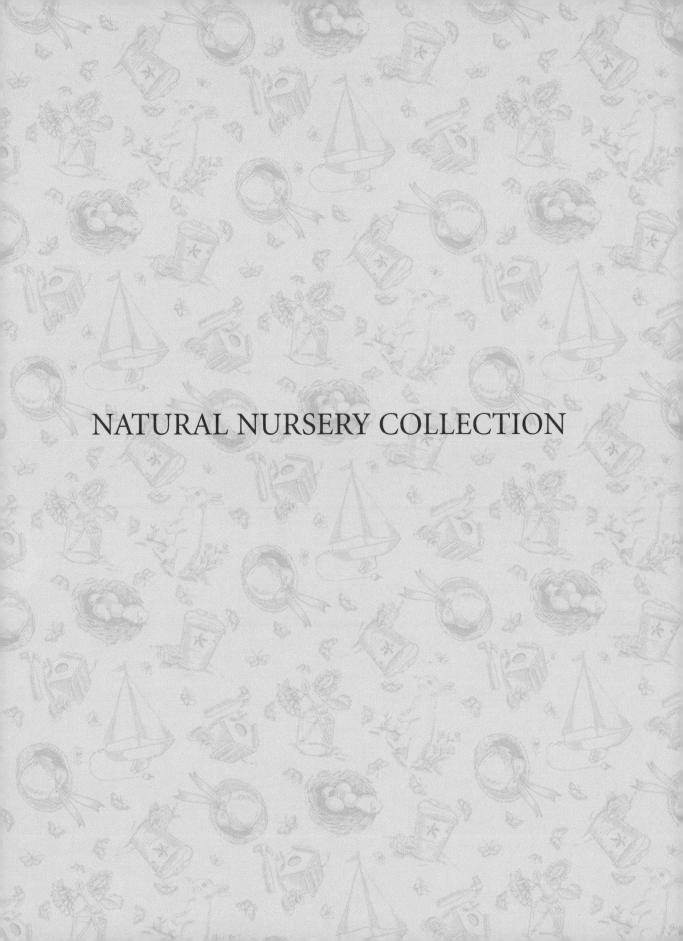

NATURAL NURSERY COLLECTION

CELLULAR BLANKET
see pages 78–79

15

TEDDY BEAR
see pages 80–83

INITIALLED WASHCLOTH
see pages 84–87

CLASSIC CARDIGAN
see pages 88–89

HARE DOORSTOP
see pages 90–93

SCENTED CUSHION
see pages 94–95

RABBIT RATTLE
see pages 96–97

33

HAT AND BOOTS
see pages 98–99

FAIRISLE PAPOOSE
see pages 100–101

FIRST BLANKET
see pages 102–103

DRESS AND PANTS
see pages 104–107

RECYCLED RAG BASKET
see pages 108–109

SWEATER AND TROUSERS
see pages 110–113

BOOTEES AND BONNET
see pages 114–117

LACE CUSHION
see pages 118–119

BIRD MOBILE
see pages 120–121

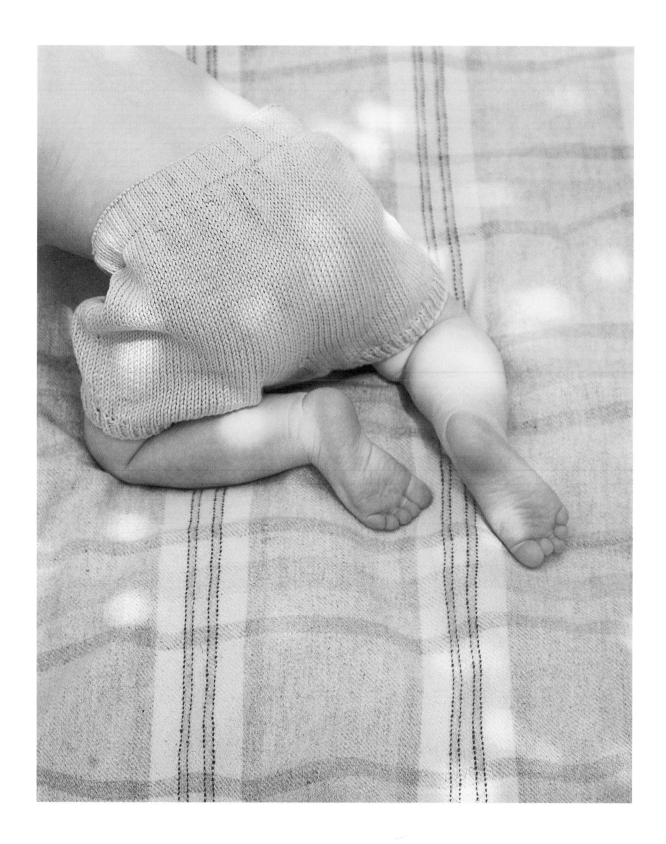

SOAKER PANTS
see pages 122–123

HEIRLOOM COT COVER
see pages 124–127

SPOTTY GIRAFFE
see pages 128–129

NIGHTIE AND HAT
see pages 130–132

NATURAL NURSERY PATTERNS

CELLULAR BLANKET

see pages 14–17

A classic project to knit as a welcome gift for a newborn baby. With a decorative open-stitch centre contrasted by a simple selvedge border, the cellular construction is both insulating and breathable, making it very comfortable for baby. The milk cotton yarn used in this project has a beautiful sheen and drape, which enhances the stitch texture. The instructions given here are for the perfect size blanket for a moses basket, crib or to cuddle into, but it can be easily made larger to suit a cot or a bed – simply cast on more stitches in multiples of four and add extra rows of the pattern.

SIZE
Approximately 68cm x 90cm

MATERIALS
7 x 50g balls of double knitting-weight milk cotton yarn, such as Rowan Milk Cotton DK in pink
Pair of 3.75mm knitting needles

TENSION
21 sts and 28 rows to 10cm square measured over patt using 3.75mm needles. Always work a tension swatch and change needles accordingly if necessary.

ABBREVIATIONS
psso pass slipped st over
skpo sl 1, k1, pass slipped st over
yo yarn over needle to make a stitch
See also page 139.

TO MAKE
Cast on 169 sts and work in rib as follows:
Rib row 1 (RS) K1, [p1, k1] to end of row.
Rib row 2 P1, [k1, p1] to end of row.
Rep these 2 rows until work measures 6.5cm, ending with RS facing for next row.
Cont in cell st patt with ribbed edges as follows:
Row 1 (RS) [K1, p1] 12 times, k3, * yo, sl 1, k2tog, psso, yo, k1; rep from * to last 26 sts, k2, [p1, k1] 12 times.
Row 2 [P1, k1] 12 times, p to last 24 sts, [k1, p1] 12 times.
Row 3 [K1, p1] 12 times, k2, k2tog, yo, k1, * yo, sl 1, k2tog, psso, yo, k1; rep from * to last 28 sts, yo, skpo, k2, [p1, k1] 12 times.
Row 4 As row 2.
These 4 rows form the patt and are repeated until work measures 83.5cm from cast-on edge, ending with RS facing for next row.
Rib row 1 (RS) K1, [p1, k1] to end of row.
Rib row 2 P1, [k1, p1] to end of row.
Rep these 2 rows for a further 6.5cm.
Cast off in rib.

TO FINISH
Weave in any yarn ends.
Lay work out flat and gently steam.

TEDDY BEAR

see pages 18–19

No nursery is complete without the traditional child's teddy bear. Knitted in garter stitch from natural British sheep breed's wool with paw pads and ears of gingham cotton fabric, this teddy bear can easily be customised to coordinate with baby's nursery.

SIZE
Approximately 36cm high

MATERIALS
3 x 100g balls of aran-weight pure wool yarn, such as Rowan Purelife British Sheep Breeds Undyed in grey-brown (A) and oddments of mid brown (B) or
R.E. Dickie British Breeds Aran Weight Natural in brown-cream marl (A) and oddments of dark brown (B)
Pair of 4mm knitting needles
Natural organic cotton stuffing
2 buttons with shanks for the eyes
Strong thread
Templates for the paw pads and ears (see page 134)
Fabric scraps, approximately 30cm square, for the paw pads and ears
Contrast yarn for the embroidery of nose and mouth
Fabric strip or ribbon for the neck tie

TENSION
22 sts and 40 rows to 10cm square measured over garter stitch, before stuffing, using 4mm needles. Always work a tension swatch and change needles accordingly if necessary.

ABBREVIATIONS
See page 139.

TIPS AND TECHNIQUES
* Worked throughout in garter st (knit every row) using 4mm needles.
* All increases are worked as kfb – knit into front and back of next st.
* When working k2tog, keep tension quite tight to avoid any holes.
* Ears, pads and paws may be knitted as given in the pattern or sewn from contrasting fabrics using the templates given (see page 134).
* If you are knitting one paw pad and sewing the other, make sure that the right side of the fabric is facing the correct way.
* Use a small amount of glue where the nose is to be stitched, this helps prevent the threads from slipping.

BODY (MAKE ONE)
Work from lower edge. With A, cast on 18 sts.
K 2 rows.
Row 3 Kfb, k7, [kfb] twice, k7, kfb. 22 sts.
Row 4 Kfb, k8, [kfb] 4 times, k8, kfb. 28 sts.
Row 5 K.
Row 6 Kfb, k11, [kfb] 4 times, K11, kfb. 34 sts.
Row 7 K.
Row 8 Kfb, k14, [kfb] 4 times, K14, kfb. 40 sts.
Row 9 Kfb, k17, [kfb] 4 times, k17, kfb. 46 sts.
Row 10 K.
Row 11 Kfb, k20, [kfb] 4 times, k20, kfb. 52 sts.
Row 12 K.
Row 13 Kfb, k23, [kfb] 4 times, k23, kfb. 58 sts.
K 10 rows.
Row 24 K2tog, k to last 2 sts, k2tog. 56 sts.
Row 25 K11, [k2tog] twice, k26, [k2tog] twice, k11. 52 sts.
Row 26 K.
Row 27 K24, [k2tog] twice, k24. 50 sts.

K 2 rows.
Row 30 K10, [k2tog] twice, k22, [k2tog] twice, k10. 46 sts.
Row 31 K21, [k2tog] twice, k21. 44 sts.
K 2 rows.
Row 34 K20, [k2tog] twice, k20. 42 sts.
Row 35 K.
Row 36 K19, [k2tog] twice, k19. 40 sts.
Row 37 K8, [k2tog] twice, k6, [k2tog] twice, k6, [k2tog] twice, k8. 34 sts.
Row 38 K.
Row 39 K15 sts, [k2tog] twice, k15. 32 sts.
Row 40 K8, k2tog, k4, [k2tog] twice, k4, k2tog, k8. 28 sts.
Row 41 K12, [k2tog] twice, k12. 26 sts.
Row 42 K6, k2tog, k3, [k2tog] twice, k3, k2tog, k6. 22 sts.
Row 43 K7, [k2tog] 4 times, k7. 18 sts.
Row 44 K2tog, k14, k2tog. 16 sts.
Row 45 K.
Row 46 K2tog, k12, k2tog. 14 sts.
Row 47 K.
Row 48 K2tog, k10, k2tog. 12 sts.
Row 49 [K2tog] 6 times. 6 sts.
Cut yarn, thread through remaining sts, pull up and fasten off.

HEAD (MAKE ONE)
Work in garter stitch.
With A, cast on 22 sts.
K 2 rows.
Row 3 K8, kfb, k4, kfb, k8. 24 sts.
K 3 rows.
Row 7 K8, kfb, k6, kfb, k8. 26 sts.
Row 8 Cast on 2 sts, k to end. 28 sts.
Row 9 Cast on 2 sts, k to end. 30 sts.
Row 10 Cast on 2 sts, k to end. 32 sts.
Row 11 Cast on 2 sts, k to end. 34 sts.

Row 12 Kfb, k11, kfb, k8, kfb, k11, kfb. 38 sts.
K 3 rows.
Row 16 K13, kfb, k10, kfb, k13. 40 sts.
Row 17 Kfb, k to last st, kfb. 42 sts.
K 5 rows.
Row 23 K14, k2tog, k10, k2tog, k14. 40 sts.
Row 24 Cast off 7 sts, k to end. 33 sts.
Row 25 Cast off 7 sts, k to end. 26 sts.
Row 26 K2tog, k5, k2tog, k8, k2tog, k5, k2tog. 22 sts.
Row 27 K2tog, k4, k2tog, k6, k2tog, k4, k2tog. 18 sts.
Row 28 K2tog, k3, k2tog, k4, k2tog, k3, k2tog. 14 sts.
Row 29 K2tog, k2, k2tog, k2, k2tog, k2, k2tog. 10 sts.
Row 30 K2tog, k6, k2tog. 8 sts.
K 5 rows.
Row 36 K2tog, k4, k2tog. 6 sts.
K 4 rows.
Row 41 K2tog, k2, k2tog. 4 sts.
K 12 rows.
Cast off.

FOOT PADS (MAKE TWO KNITTED OR ONE IF MAKING IN FABRIC)
With B, cast on 6 sts.
Row 1 K.
Rows 2, 3 and 4 Kfb, k to last st, kfb. 12 sts.
K 14 rows.
Row 19 K2tog, k8, k2tog. 10 sts.
K 13 rows.
Row 33 K2tog, k to last 2 sts, k2tog.
Row 34 K.
Rows 35 to 42 Rep rows 33 and 34 four more times.
Cast off.

LEGS (MAKE TWO)
Start at foot. With A, cast on 48 sts.
K 6 rows.

Row 7 K18, [k2tog] 6 times, k18. 42 sts.
Row 8 K.
Row 9 K15, [k2tog] 6 times, k15. 36 sts.
Row 10 K.
Row 11 K12, [k2tog] 6 times, k12. 30 sts.
Row 12 K.
Row 13 K2tog, k7, [k2tog] 6 times, k7, k2tog. 22 sts.
Row 14 K.
Row 15 K5, [k2tog] 6 times, k5. 16 sts.
K 24 rows.
Row 40 Kfb, k6, [kfb] twice, k6, kfb. 20 sts.
Row 41 K.
Row 42 Kfb, k8, [kfb] twice, k8, kfb. 24 sts.
Rows 43 and 44 K.
Row 45 K2tog, k8, [k2tog] twice, k8, k2tog. 20 sts.
Row 46 K.
Row 47 K2tog, k6, [k2tog] twice, k6, k2tog. 16 sts.
Row 48 K2tog, k4, [k2tog] twice, k4, k2tog. 12 sts.
Row 49 K2tog, k2, [k2tog] twice, k2, k2tog. 8 sts.
Row 50 [K2tog] 4 times. 4 sts.
Row 51 [K2tog] twice. 2 sts.
Cut yarn, thread through last st, pull up and fasten off.

EARS (IF FABRIC LINED, MAKE TWO IN A;
IF KNITTED, MAKE TWO IN A AND TWO IN B)
Cast on 10 sts.
K 10 rows.
Row 11 K2tog, k6, k2tog. 8 sts.
K 1 row.
Row 13 K2tog, k4, k2tog. 6 sts.
K 1 row.
Cast off, working k2tog at each end of row.

ARMS (MAKE TWO)
Start at paw. With A, cast on 4 sts.

Row 1 K.
Row 2 Kfb, k2, kfb. 6 sts.
K 3 rows.
Row 6 Kfb, k4, kfb. 8 sts.
K 3 rows.
Row 10 Kfb, k6, kfb. 10 sts.
SHAPE PAW
Row 11 K2tog, k to last st, kfb. 10 sts.
K 3 rows.
Row 15 K.
Row 16 K2tog, k to last st, kfb. 10 sts.
K 3 rows.
Row 20 Cast on 10 sts, k to end. 20 sts.
Row 21 K2tog, k7, [kfb] twice, k7, k2tog. 20 sts.
K 3 rows.
Row 25 K2tog, k7, [kfb] twice, k7. k2tog. 20 sts.
K 3 rows.
Row 29 K2tog, k7, [kfb] twice, k7, k2tog. 20 sts.
K 21 rows.
SHAPE TOP OF ARM
Row 51 K2tog, k6, [k2tog] twice, k6, k2tog. 16 sts.
K 2 rows.
Row 54 K2tog, k4, [k2tog] twice, k4, k2tog. 12 sts.
Rows 55 and 56 Knit.
Row 57 K2tog, k2, [k2tog] twice, k2, k2tog. 8 sts.
Row 58 [K2tog] 4 times. 4 sts.
Row 59 [K2tog] twice. 2 sts.
Row 60 K2tog.
Cut yarn, thread through last st, pull up and fasten off.

PAW PADS (MAKE TWO IN B)
Work rows 1 to 19 of arm pattern then cast off.

TO MAKE UP
Sew each piece together firmly using small back stitches, but leave a small opening for stuffing.

Stuff firmly, but avoid distorting the limbs, and then stitch the opening.

Attach the head to the body using ladder stitch, which can be drawn up tightly until the head is as firmly secured as required.

Attach the limbs to the body using thread jointing, using strong thread making a moveable joint.

Attach the eyes to the head using strong thread as follows:

Using a long double thread pass the thread through the eye loop and tie securely in the centre. Thread the four threads onto a darning needle and pass through the required eye position and out through the back of the neck.

Unthread two of the four threads, take a small stitch (about 3mm) with the remaining two threads and then unthread these two and tie securely to the first two threads, pulling the eye into the head to the desired depth, knot several times and fasten off, by passing the threads inside the head before cutting.

Attach the ears in the required position using ladder stitch, so as to be able to pull the ears into the required shape.

Embroider the nose and mouth using a contrasting yarn.

* If you are making one knitted paw pad and one in fabric, ensure you cut the fabric with the right side appropriate to the arm you chose – ie. left or right.

INITIALLED WASHCLOTH

see pages 20–21

A simple washcloth, knitted in natural hemp yarn, which can be personalised with an initial worked in reverse stocking stitch. Wrapped up with a piece of handmade organic soap, this washcloth makes a practical yet inexpensive gift.

SIZE
Approximately 30cm x 30cm square

MATERIALS
1 x 100g skein of double-knitting-weight yarn, such as Lanaknits Allhemp6 DK in green
Pair of 3.75mm knitting needles
15cm of 1.5cm wide cotton gingham ribbon and one press stud (optional)
Contrast colour cotton embroidery thread (optional)

TENSION
22 sts and 26 rows to 10cm square over st st using 3.75mm needles. Always work a tension swatch and change needles accordingly if necessary.

ABBREVIATIONS
See page 139.

TIPS AND TECHNIQUES
* Each letter is worked from a chart, 24 sts wide and 32 rows long, and is placed as given in the pattern instructions. See pages 85–87 for the complete set of alphabet charts.

TO MAKE
Cast on 66 sts.
K 2 rows.
Next row (RS) K.
Next row K2, p to last 2 sts, k2.
Rep the last 2 rows 10 times more.
PLACE LETTER CHART
Row 1 (RS) K21, work across 24 sts of 1st row of chart, k21.
Row 2 K2, p19, work across 24 sts of 2nd row of chart, p19, k2.
These 2 rows place the position of the chart and are repeated, working the correct chart rows, until all 32 rows have been completed and RS of work is facing for next row.
Beg with a k row, work a further 21 rows in st st with garter stitch edge as set, ending with WS facing for next row.
K 2 rows.
Cast off.

TO FINISH
Weave in any yarn ends.
Lay work out flat and gently steam.
The washcloth can either be left plain or a blanket stitch edging can be worked around all sides using a contrasting coloured cotton embroidery thread.
To make a hanging loop, thread the gingham ribbon through the washcloth, approximately 3cm in from one corner, fold the ends in to neaten the ribbon and sew the press stud in place.

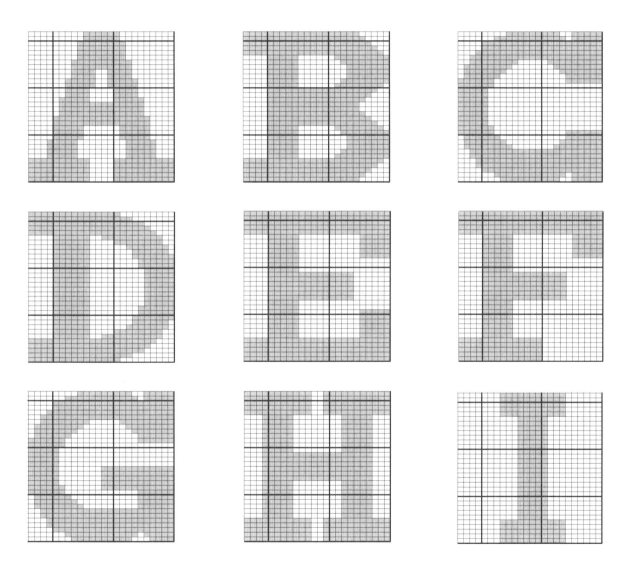

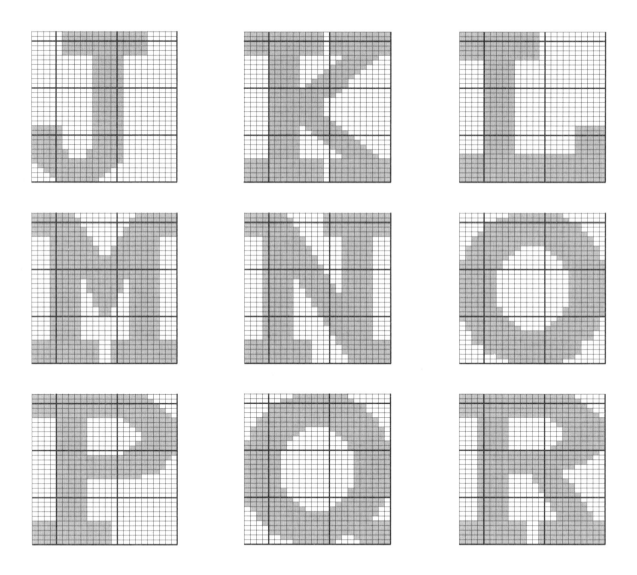

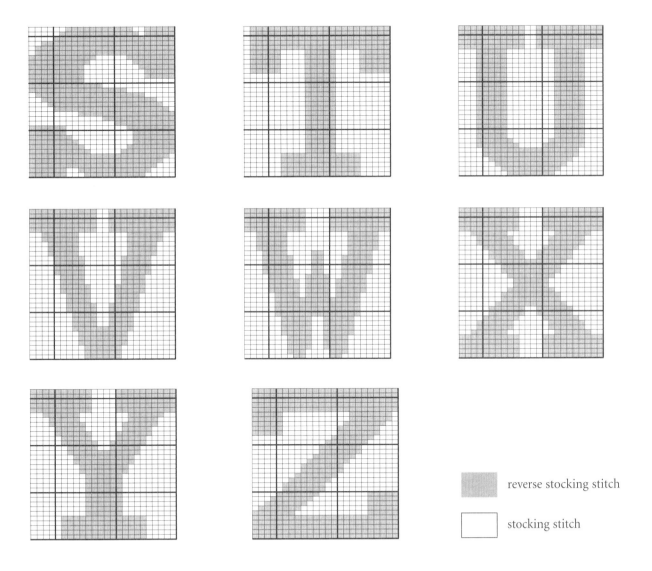

reverse stocking stitch

stocking stitch

CLASSIC CARDIGAN

see pages 22–23

Worked in one piece for maximum ease for the knitter and comfort for the wearer, this simple cardigan is made in the softest baby alpaca yarn. This design combines integral rib edges and press stud fastenings for a modern, practical touch.

SIZE
To fit newborn (0–3: 3–6) months
Chest 38 (43: 49)cm
Length 38 (42: 46)cm
Sleeve length 7 (8: 9)cm

MATERIALS
2 (2: 3) x 50g balls of double-knitting-weight alpaca yarn, such as Rowan Classic Baby Alpaca DK in cream, brown or grey
Pair each of 3.75mm and 4mm knitting needles
4 natural horn buttons (preferably from a sustainable source)
4 press studs

TENSION
22 sts and 30 rows to 10cm square over st st using 4mm needles. Always work a tension swatch and change needles accordingly if necessary.

ABBREVIATIONS
See page 139.

TIPS AND TECHNIQUES
* For neatness, join in new balls of yarn at the sides, not at the front edges.

BACK
Using 3.75 needles, cast on 44 (50: 56) sts.
Row 1 (RS) K2, [p1, k2] to end of row.
Row 2 P2, [k1, p2] to end of row.
These 2 rows form the rib and are repeated twice more.
Change to 4mm needles.
Beg with a k row, work in st st until back measures 10.5 (12: 13.5)cm from cast-on edge, ending with RS facing for next row.

SHAPE SLEEVES
Next row (RS) Cast on 18 (20: 22) sts loosely at beg of row and work as follows: [p1, k2] twice, p1, k to end of row.
Next row Cast on 18 (20: 22) sts loosely at beg of row and work row as follows: [k1, p2] twice, k1, p to last 7 sts, [k1, p2] twice, k1. 80 (90: 100) sts.
Cont straight in st st with rib edges as set until work measures 17 (19: 21)cm from cast-on edge, ending with RS facing for next row.
Next row P1, [k2, p1] twice, k19 (21: 23), [p1, k2] 9 (11: 13) times, p1, k19 (21: 23), [p1, k2] twice, p1.
Next row K1, [p2, k1] twice, p19 (21: 23), [k1, p2] 9 (11: 13) times, k1, p19 (21: 23), [k1, p2] twice, k1.
Rep the last 2 rows once more.

SHAPE RIGHT FRONT SLOPE AND SLEEVE
Next row (RS) P1, [k2, p1] twice, k19 (21: 23), [p1, k2] twice, p1, turn and leave rem sts on a holder.
Next row K1, [p2, k1] twice, p19 (21: 23), [k1, p2] twice, k1.
Next row (inc) P1, [k2, p1] twice, k to last 9 sts, m1, k2, [p1, k2] twice, p1.
Inc 1 st at neck edge as set on every foll alt row until there are 44 (44: 46) sts.
2ND AND 3RD SIZES ONLY
Inc 1 st at neck edge as set on every row until there are – (49: 54) sts.

Cont straight until sleeve measures 17 (18: 19)cm in width, ending at cuff edge.

Next row Cast off 18 (20: 22) sts and cont on rem 26 (29: 32) sts until work measures 36 (40: 44)cm from cast on edge, ending with RS facing for next row and inc 1 st at end of last row. 27 (30: 33) sts.
Change to 3.75mm needles and work 6 rows in rib as follows:
Row 1 (RS) [K2, p1] to end of row.
Row 2 [K1, p2] to end of row.
Cast off in rib.
With RS facing and 4mm needles, rejoin yarn to rem sts, cast off 14 (20: 26) sts at centre back in rib, rib the next 6 sts as set, k to last 7 sts, p1, [k2, p1] to end of row.

SHAPE LEFT FRONT SLOPE AND SLEEVE
Next row (WS) K1, [p2, k1] twice, p19 (21: 23), [k1, p2] twice, k1.
Next row (inc) P1, [k2, p1] twice, k2, m1, k to last 7 sts, [p1, k2] twice, p1.
Inc 1 st at neck edge as set on every foll alt row until there are 44 (44: 46) sts.

2ND AND 3RD SIZES ONLY
Inc 1 st at neck edge as set on every row until – (49: 54) sts.

ALL SIZES
Cont straight until sleeve measures 17 (18: 19)cm in width, ending at cuff edge.

Next row Cast off 18 (20: 22) sts and cont on rem 26 (29: 32) sts until work measures 36 (40: 44)cm from cast-on edge, ending with RS facing for next row and inc 1 st at beg of last row. 27 (30: 33) sts.
Change to 3.75mm needles and work 6 rows rib as follows:
Row 1 (RS) [P1, k2] to end of row.

Row 2 [P2, k1] to end of row.
Cast off in rib.

POCKETS (MAKE 2)
Using 3.75mm needles, cast on 11 sts.
Beg with a k row, work 2 rows in st st.
Next row K3, m1, k to last 3 sts, m1, k3. 13 sts.
P 1 row.
Rep the last 2 rows once more. 15 sts.
Work 8 rows straight, ending with RS facing for next row.
Work 2 rows in rib as follows:
Row 1 K1, [p1, k2] to last 2 sts, p1, k1.
Row 2 P1, [k1, p2], to last 2 sts, k1, p1.
Cast off in rib.

TO FINISH
Weave in any yarn ends.
Lay work out flat and gently steam.
Sew side and sleeve seams.
Sew on pockets.
Sew press studs to front ribbed bands, then sew buttons above press studs to detail.

HARE DOORSTOP

see pages 24–25

A practical and adorable doorstop for the nursery, a sitting hare. Knitted in stocking stitch from natural hemp yarn, with one floppy ear acting as a puller, the hare is stuffed with organic cotton and natural rice grains to act as ballast.

SIZE
Approximately 35cm from tip of ear to base

MATERIALS
1 x 100g skein of double-knitting-weight yarn, such as Lanaknits Allhemp6 DK in ecru
Pair of 3.25mm knitting needles
0.5m of muslin for lining
Dry rice (or small dry lentils) for stuffing
Organic cotton stuffing
Small piece of cardboard
Oddments of mid-brown wool for pompon tail

TENSION
22 sts and 30 rows to 10cm square over st st using 3.25mm needles. Always work a tension swatch and change needles accordingly if necessary.

ABBREVIATIONS
See page 139.

TIPS AND TECHNIQUES
* When you have made and checked your tension swatch, unravel it and use the yarn to work the base – you may need an extra skein of yarn if you do not re-use the swatch.
* Both a chart and written instruction are given for this project, chose whichever method you prefer.

* When working from a chart work even numbered rows from right to left and odd numbered rows from left to right.
* Each square represents one st and one row.
* The hare is worked throughout in st st and comprises 2 sides, 1 base and 2 inner ears.
* On Side 1 all odd-numbered rows are k, all even-numbered rows are p. On Side 2 all odd-numbered rows are p, all even-numbered rows are k.
* All incs and decs are k or p twice into st and are worked one st in from the edge.
* Side 1: all decs are worked k2tog or p2tog.
* Side 2: all decs are worked k2tog tbl or p2tog tbl.

SIDE (MAKE TWO – SEE TIPS AND TECHNIQUES)
Cast on 45 sts and work in st st as follows:
(Side 1 will beg with a k row and side 2 will beg with a p row.)
Rows 1 and 2 Work 2 rows.
Row 3 Inc 1 st at end of row. 46 sts.
Row 4 Work 1 row.
Row 5 Inc 1 st at end of row. 47 sts.
Row 6 Work 1 row.
Row 7 Dec 1 st at beg of row. 46 sts.
Row 8 Work 1 row.
Row 9 Dec 1 st at beg and inc 1 st at end of row. 46 sts.
Row 10 Dec 1 st at end of row. 45 sts.
Row 11 Cast off 3 sts at beg of row. 42 sts.
Row 12 Dec 1 st at end of row. 41 sts.
Row 13 Cast off 2 sts at beg and dec 1 st at end of row. 38 sts.
Row 14 Cast off 3 sts at beg and dec 1 st at end of row. 34 sts.
Row 15 Dec 1 st at end of row. 33 sts.
Row 16 Work 1 row.
Row 17 Dec 1 st at beg of row. 32 sts.

Row 18 Inc 1 st at beg of row. 33 sts.
Row 19 Work 1 row.
Row 20 Inc 1 st at beg of row. 34 sts.
Rows 21 and 22 Work 2 rows.
Row 23 Inc 1 st each end of row. 36 sts.
Row 24 Inc 1 st at end of row. 37 sts.
Row 25 Inc 1 st at beg of row. 38 sts.
Row 26 Inc 1 st at beg of row. 39 sts.
Row 27 Inc 1 st at beg of row. 40 sts.
Row 28 and 29 Work 2 rows.
Row 30 Inc 1 st at beg of row. 41 sts.
Row 31 Inc 1 st at beg of row. 42 sts.
Rows 32 and 33 Work 2 rows.
Row 34 Inc 1 st at end of row. 43 sts.
Rows 35, 36 and 37 Work 3 rows.
Rows 38 Dec 1 st at beg of row and inc 1 st at end of row. 43 sts.
Row 39 Work 1 row.
Row 40 Dec 1 st at beg of row. 42 sts.
Row 41 Inc 1 st at beg of row and dec 1 st at end of row. 42 sts.
Row 42 Work 1 row.
Row 43 Dec 1 st at end of row. 41 sts.
Row 44 work 1 row.
Row 45 Inc 1 st at beg of row and dec 1 st at end of row. 41 sts.
Row 46 Dec 1 st at beg of row. 40 sts.
Row 47 Dec 1 st at end of row. 39 sts.
Row 48 Dec 1 st at beg of row. 38 sts.
Row 49 Cast on 5 sts at beg of row and dec 1 st at end of row. 42 sts.
Row 50 Dec 1 st at beg of row and inc 1 st at end of row. 42 sts.
Row 51 Inc 1 st at beg of row and dec 1 st at end of row. 42 sts.
Row 52 Dec 1 st at beg of row and inc 1 st at end of row. 42 sts.

Row 53 Dec 1 st at end of row. 41 sts.
Row 54 Dec 1 st at beg of row. 40 sts.
Row 55 Dec 1 st at end of row. 39 sts.
Row 56 Cast off 4 sts at beg of row. 35 sts.
Row 57 Dec 1 st at end of row. 34 sts.
Row 58 Cast off 4 sts at beg of row. 30 sts.
Row 59 Dec 1 st at each end of row. 28 sts.
Row 60 Cast off 3 sts at beg of row. 25 sts.
Row 61 Dec 1 st at end of row. 24 sts.
Row 62 Cast off 2 sts at beg of row and dec 1 st at end of row. 21 sts.
Row 63 Dec 1 st each end of row. 19 sts.
Row 64 Cast off 2 sts at beg of row. 17 sts.
Row 65 Dec 1 st each end of row. 15 sts.
Row 66 Dec 1 st at beg of row. 14 sts.
Row 67 Dec 1 st at beg of row. 13 sts.
Row 68 Dec 1 st at end of row. 12 sts.
Row 69 Dec 1 st at beg of row and inc 1 st at end of row. 12 sts.
Row 70 Dec 1 st at end of row. 11 sts.
Row 71 Dec 1 st at beg of row and inc 1 st at end of row. 11 sts.
Row 72 Work 1 row.
Row 73 Inc 1 st at end of row. 12 sts.
Row 74 Inc 1 st at beg of row and dec 1 st at end of row. 12 sts.
Row 75 Work 1 row.
Row 76: Inc 1 st at beg of row and dec 1 st at end of row. 12 sts.
Row 77 Inc 1 st at end of row. 13 sts.
Row 78 Dec 1 st at end of row. 12 sts.
Row 79 Work 1 row.
Row 80 Inc 1 st at beg of row and dec 1 st at end of row. 12 sts.
Rows 81 and 82 Work 2 rows.

Row 83 Inc 1 st at end of row. 13 sts.
Row 84 Dec 1 st at end of row. 12 sts.
Rows 85 and 86 Work 2 rows.
Row 87 Inc 1 st at end of row. 13 sts.
Rows 88 and 89 Work 2 rows.
Row 90 Dec 1 st at end of row. 12 sts.
Row 91 Inc 1 st at end of row. 13 sts.
Rows 92 and 93 Work 2 rows.
Row 94 Dec 1 st at end of row. 12 sts.
Row 95 Work 1 row.
Row 96 Dec 1 st at end of row. 11 sts.
Row 97 Dec 1 st at beg of row. 10 sts.
Row 98 Dec 1 st each end of row. 8 sts.
Row 99 Work 1 row.
Row 100 Dec 1 st at end of row. 7 sts.
Row 101 Dec 1 st at beg of row. 6 sts.
Row 102 Dec 1 st each end of row. 4 sts.
Row 103 Dec 1 st at beg of row. 3 sts.
Row 104 Work 3 sts tog.
Fasten off.

BASE (MAKE ONE)
Cast on 4 sts and beg with a k row, work in st st
as follows:
Inc 1 st at each end of 3rd and every foll alt row until
there are 20 sts.
Work 25 rows straight, so ending with RS facing for
next row.
Dec 1 st at each end of next row and every foll alt
rows until 4 sts rem.
Work 1 row.
Cast off.

EARS (MAKE TWO)
Cast on 17 sts and beg with a k row, work from row
65 of main pattern and work to end.

TO MAKE INNER LINING
Lay one side piece and base onto paper and draw
around each piece (excluding ears), adding 1cm
for seams.
From lining fabric, cut two side pieces and one
base piece.
Seam around back, head and front of lining.
Sew on base, leaving opening for stuffing/rice.
Cut one base piece in card.
Stuff head and top of hare fully with organic stuffing.
Pour in rice to fill base of inner lining.
Attach base, leaving an opening then insert card into
base and stitch up opening.

TAIL (MAKE ONE)
Cut two circles of cardboard 5cm in diameter.
Cut a hole in the centre of each one and hold the
circles together.
Thread a blunt-ended yarn needle with yarn and
wind it continually through the centre and outer
edges until the hole has closed.
Insert the tips of scissors between the two circles and
cut the yarn around the cardboard circles.
Tie a piece of yarn tightly between the two cardboard
circles. Remove the cardboard, cutting through them
if necessary.
Trim any uneven strands for a neat finish.

TO MAKE UP
Weave in any yarn ends.
Lay work out flat and gently steam.
Oversew around head and body, evenly stuff both
ears with organic cotton.
Attach base leaving an opening for lining.
Insert lining and stitch up opening.
Sew pompon to back seam for tail.

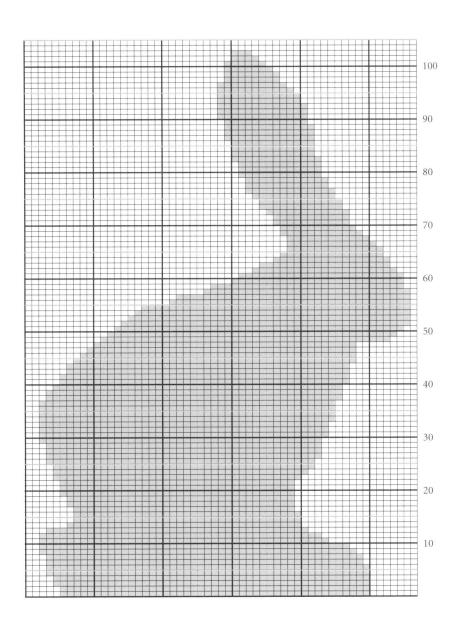

100

90

80

70

60

50

40

30

20

10

SCENTED CUSHION

see pages 28–31

A tiny cushion that is the perfect size to hang on the nursery door handle to prevent it from banging and waking up baby. Knitted in crisp mercerised cotton, the gingham design is worked in three colours and then backed with natural linen, trimmed with a picot edge and finished with a mother of pearl button or dried rosebud. Filling the cushion is a scented sachet of either lavender or rose, which may help baby to drift off to sleep.

SIZE
Approximately 14cm x 14cm square including edging

MATERIALS
Small amounts of fine-weight 4ply mercerised cotton yarn, such as Yeoman's Cotton Cannele 4ply in cream, light green and dark green
Pair of 2.75mm knitting needles
2mm crochet hook
30cm x 25cm piece of natural linen fabric
45cm of 1.5cm wide cotton tape
Organza fabric approximately 26cm x 14cm
Dried lavender or rosebuds for scented sachet
Optional mother of pearl button or dried rosebud

TENSION
34 sts and 34 rows to 10cm square over pattern using 2.75mm needles. Always work a tension swatch and change needles accordingly if necessary.

ABBREVIATIONS
See page 139.

GINGHAM PATTERN
Multiple of 8 sts
Row 1 (RS) K3A, [2B, 2A] to last st, 1A.
Row 2 P3A, [2B, 2A] to last st, 1A.
Row 3 K3B, [2C, 2B] to last st, 1B.
Row 4 P3B, [2C, 2B] to last st, 1B.
These 4 rows form the pattern and are repeated.

TO MAKE CUSHION
Using yarn A and 2.75mm needles, cast on 48 sts and work 12.5 cm in gingham pattern, ending with RS facing for next row.
Cast off.

TO FINISH
Weave in any yarn ends.
Lay work out flat and gently steam.

EDGING
Work a simple picot edging using cream yarn as follows:
With RS facing and beg in the centre of one edge, work: 1dc, * 3ch, ss into 3rd ch from hook (1 picot worked), miss next st or row end, 1dc into next st or row end; rep from * along each side, working 2 picot into each corner.
Join with a ss into 1st dc worked.
Fasten off.

CUSHION BACK
Cut a piece of natural linen, 14.5cm x 9cm for upper back and another, 14.5cm x 13cm for lower back.
On one 14.5cm edge of each piece, fold and press a 5mm then 1cm hem and topstitch in place.
Fold 1cm on remaining 3 sides of each piece onto the wrong side and press.

For the hanging loop, fold tape in half, and pin to the centre of the wrong side of top edge of square.
With wrong sides together, lay lower back piece onto knitted square and slipstitch in place around the edge. Lay upper back piece onto wrong side of knitted square over the lower back piece and slipstitch in place around the edge, securing tape in the seam.
Sew button or rosebud to centre of square.

SCENTED SACHET
Fold organza fabric in half across the width and taking a 1cm seam, stitch around two open edges and 3cm of the third edge. Turn through to right side, fill with dried lavender or rosebuds and slipstitch the remaining part of third edge. Insert sachet into cushion cover.

RABBIT RATTLE

see pages 32–33

Soft bracelet rattle with little rabbit head made in baby alpaca yarn, with simple embroidery and ribbon detail.

SIZE
Approximately 8cm in diameter

MATERIALS
1 x 50g ball of double-knitting-weight organic cotton, such as Rowan Purelife Organic Cotton Naturally Dyed DK in ecru and oddments in grey
Pair each size 3mm and 4mm knitting needles
Small bell
Oddments of yarn for embroidery
Small amount of natural organic cotton stuffing
20cm of 1.5cm wide ribbon

TENSION
25 sts and 35 rows to 10cm square over st st using 3mm needles. Always work a tension swatch and change needles accordingly if necessary.

ABBREVIATIONS
See page 139.

RATTLE RING
Using 4mm needles, cast on 26 sts.
Change to 3mm needles and work as follows:
Row 1 (RS) [K1, inc in next st] to end of row. 39 sts.
Beg with a p row work 3 rows in st st.
Row 5 [K2, inc in next st] to end of row. 52 sts.
Beg with a p row work 13 rows in st st.
Row 19 [K2, k2tog] to end of row. 39 sts.
Beg with a p row work 3 rows in st st.
Row 23 [K1, k2tog] to end of row. 26 sts.
Cast off using 4mm needles.

HEAD
With 3mm needles, cast on 16 sts.
Row 1 P.
Row 2 [K1, inc in next stitch] to end. 24 sts.
Beg with a p row, work 12 rows in st st.
Row 15 [P2tog] to end of row. 12 sts.
Cut yarn, thread through rem sts and pull up and fasten off.
Join seam, leaving cast on edge open, stuff firmly with bell inserted in the centre.
Run a thread around cast-on edge, pull up and secure.

EARS (MAKE 2)
Cast on 11 sts.
Beg with a k row, work 2 rows in st st.
Cont in st st and dec 1 st at each end of next row and 3 foll RS rows.
Next row P3tog.
Fasten off.

TO FINISH
Join row ends of ring, using mattress st.
Graft the cast-on and cast-off edges together, pushing stuffing into the rattle as you work.
Sew ears onto head and sew head to rattle.
Embroider face as shown.
Tie ribbon around neck.

HAT AND BOOTS

see pages 34–35

The perfect hat and boots set for top-to-toe style. A simple pull-on hat worked in stripes of green and ecru with rolled brim is complemented by the plain and easy boots knitted in stocking stitch in contrast rib cuffs and pull-on tabs.

SIZE
To fit 0–3 (3–6: 6–9) months
Length of boot 8 (9: 10) cm

MATERIALS
2 x 50g balls of double-knitting-weight organic cotton, such as Rowan Purelife Organic Cotton Naturally Dyed DK in green (A) and 1 x 50g ball in ecru (B)
Pair each 3.25 and 3.75 mm knitting needles
20cm of 1cm wide cotton tape

TENSION
22 sts and 30 rows to 10cm square over st st using 3.75mm needles. Always work a tension swatch and change needles accordingly if necessary.

ABBREVIATIONS
See page 139.

HAT

COLOUR SEQUENCE
11 rows A.
1 row B.
7 rows A.
3 rows B.
5 rows A.
5 rows B.
3 rows A.
10 rows B.
2 rows A.
8 rows B.
2 rows A.
5 rows B.

TO MAKE
Using 3.25 mm needles and A, cast on 73 (82: 91) sts.
Beg with a k row and following the colour sequence above, work 6 rows in st st.
Change to 3.75 mm needles and cont in stripe pattern until work measures 14 (15: 16)cm from cast-on edge, ending with RS facing for next row.
SHAPE TOP
Row 1 (RS) [K7, k2tog] to last st, k1. 65 (73: 81) sts.
Row 2 P.
Row 3 [K6, k2tog] to last st, k1. 57 (64: 71) sts.
Row 4 P.
Row 5 [K5, k2tog] to last st, k1. 49 (55: 61) sts.
Row 6 P.
Row 7 [K4, k2tog] to last st, k1. 41 (46: 51) sts.
Row 8 P.
Row 9 [K3, k2tog] to last st, k1. 33 (37: 41) sts.
Row 10 P.
Row 11 [K2, k2tog] to last st, k1. 25 (28: 31) sts.
Row 12 P.

Row 13 [K1, k2tog] to last st, k1. 17 (19: 21) sts.
Row 14 [K2tog] to last st, k1. 9 (10: 11) sts.

TO FINISH
Cut yarn leaving a long end and thread through rem sts. Pull up tightly and secure the join seam, reversing seam at lower edge to allow brim to roll.
Weave in any yarn ends.
Gently steam.

BOOTS

SOLE
Using 3.25mm needles and A, cast on 32 (38: 44) sts and beg with a k row work in st st, shaping as follows:
Row 1 (RS) K2, m1, k13 (16: 19), m1, k2, m1, k13 (16: 19), m1, k2. 36 (42: 48) sts.
Row 2 P.
Row 3 K2, m1, k15 (18: 21), m1, k2, m1, k15 (18: 21), m1, k2. 40 (46: 52) sts.
Row 4 P.
Row 5 K2, m1, k17 (20: 23), m1, k2, m1, k17 (20: 23), m1, k2. 44 (50: 56) sts.
Row 6 P.
Ridge Row P.
UPPER
Beg with a p row, work 5 (7: 7) rows in st st, so ending with RS facing for next row.
SHAPE FOOT
Row 1 K20 (23: 26) sts, k2tog tbl, k2tog, k to end. 42 (48: 54) sts.
Row 2 P19 (22: 25) sts, p2tog, p2tog tbl, p to end. 40 (46: 52) sts.
Row 3 K18 (21: 24) sts, k2tog tbl, k2tog, k to end.

38 (44: 50) sts.
Row 4 P17 (20: 23) sts, p2tog, p2tog tbl, p to end. 36 (42: 48) sts.
Row 5 K16 (19: 22) sts, k2tog tbl, k2tog, k to end. 34 (40: 46) sts.
Row 6 P15 (18: 21) sts, p2tog, p2tog tbl, p to end. 32 (38: 44) sts.
Row 7 K14 (17: 20) sts, k2tog tbl, k2tog, k to end. 30 (36: 42) sts.
Row 8 P.
Row 9 K13 (16: 19) sts, k2tog tbl, k2tog, k to end. 28 (34: 40) sts.
Row 10 P.
Row 11 [K1, p1] to end of row.
The last row forms rib and is repeated 13 (17: 22) times more.
Cast off loosely but evenly in rib.

TO FINISH
Fold cast-on edge in half and join seam to form sole.
Join back seam from sole to ankle.
Fold rib in half onto wrong side and slip stitch in place.
Cut tape in half, now fold each piece in half to form a loop and attach to the inside back seam at lower edge of ribbing.

FAIRISLE PAPOOSE

see pages 38–39

The simplest and most stylish project to make for a new baby. Knitted in a single strip of stocking stitch, the piece is then folded and sewn, finished with a ribbed edge and topped off with a fluffy pompon. It makes a snug and practical 'bag' to pop baby into whether they are in the crib, stroller or being held in your arms. The fairisle is kept simple by being worked in only two colours, but this project is just as effective when knitted in a single colour with a contrast rib edge.

SIZE
Length approximately 70cm to top of hood

MATERIALS
6 x 50g balls of double-knitting-weight organic cotton, such as Rowan Purelife Organic Cotton Naturally Dyed DK in pink (A) and 2 x 50g balls in grey (B)
Pair 2.75mm knitting needles
One 3.25mm circular needle

TENSION
22 sts and 30 rows to 10cm square over st st pattern using 3.75mm needles. Always work a tension swatch and change needles accordingly if necessary.

ABBREVIATIONS
See page 139.

CHART NOTES
* The chart is worked over 90 sts and 60 rows, which are repeated.
* Strand yarn not in use across WS of work, weaving in every 2–3 sts.
* Use separate balls of yarn for each motif on chart rows 13–21, twisting yarn at colour change to avoid holes.

BACK
Using yarn A and 2.75mm needles, cast on 90 sts. Beg with a k row, work 210 rows in st st from chart, so ending with row 30 of 4th repeat. Cast off.

FRONT
Using yarn A and 2.75mm needles, cast on 90 sts. Beg with a k row, work 150 rows in st st from chart, so ending with row 30 of 3rd repeat. Cast off.

TO MAKE UP
Fold cast-on edge of Back in half and join seam to form top edge of hood. Matching patterns and using mattress stitch, join side seams from cast-off edges of back and front up to cast-on edge of front. Join cast-off edges of front to back to form lower edge of papoose.

EDGING
Using 3.25mm circular needle and yarn B, pick up and k90 sts across cast-on edge of front, 57 sts up row ends of back to hood seam and 57 sts down row ends of back to cast-on edge of front. 204 sts. Working in rows not rounds, work 5 rows in k1, p1 rib. Cast off in rib. Join edging seam.

TO FINISH
Weave in any yarn ends. Make a 6cm pompon (see page 90) from yarn B and sew to point of hood.

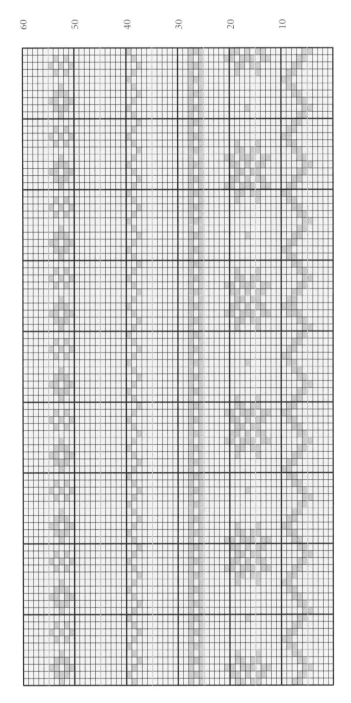

A pink

B grey

101

FIRST BLANKET

see pages 40–41

This elegant blanket is the ideal gift to welcome a new baby into the world. Made in exquisite natural bamboo yarn, the main basic garter stitch is complemented by a simple decorative edging. Tie the folded blanket with a sumptuous cotton velvet bow and then wrap in tissue paper for a memorable gift.

SIZE
Approximately 85cm x 106cm (including edging)

MATERIALS
15 x 50g balls of double-knitting-weight natural bamboo yarn, Rowan RYC Bamboo Soft in silver-grey
Pair of 3.75mm knitting needles

TENSION
22 sts and 42 rows to 10cm square over garter st using 3.75mm needles. Always work a tension swatch and change needles accordingly if necessary.

ABBREVIATIONS
See page 139.

MAIN PIECE
Cast on 175 sts and work 100cm in garter st.
Cast off.

EDGING
Cast on 5 sts.
Row 1 (RS) K.
Row 2 K2, m1, k3.
Row 3 K4, m1, k2.
Row 4 K3, m1, k4.
Row 5 K5, m1, k3.
Row 6 Cast off 4 sts, k to end.
Rep these 6 rows until work measures approximately 3.65m, ending with row 5.
Next row Cast off all sts.

TO FINISH
Weave in any yarn ends.
Slip stitch edging to main piece, gently gathering edging around corners.

DRESS AND PANTS

see pages 42–45

A basic little dress and pants set made in a fine milk cotton yarn. The dress is knitted in plain stocking stitch, with picot-edge details to cuff and hem, and has a practical and neat open back that ties with linen tapes. The pants are worked in simple garter stitch with a linen tape that ties at the waist.

SIZE
To fit 0–3 (3–6: 6–9) months
Dress
Chest 48 (51: 55)cm
Length to shoulder 30.5 (33: 35.5)cm
Sleeve length 14.5 (15.5: 16.5)cm

MATERIALS
Dress 4 (4: 5) x 50g balls of 4ply-weight milk cotton yarn, such as Rowan Fine Milk Cotton in beige
Pants 2 x 50g balls of 4ply-weight milk cotton yarn, such as Rowan Fine Milk Cotton in beige
Pair each of 2.25mm and 2.75mm knitting needles
2m of 1.5cm wide linen tape

TENSIONS
27 sts and 54 rows over garter st and 29 sts and 38 rows over st st both to 10cm square using 2.75mm needles. Always work a tension swatch and change needles accordingly if necessary.

ABBREVIATIONS
See page 139.

TIPS AND TECHNIQUES
Garter stitch pants are worked in one piece from the front waistband, with the back waist shaped with short rows.

DRESS

FRONT
With 2.75mm needles, cast on 102 (108: 114) sts.
Beg with a k row, work 4 rows in st st.
Next row (picot hem) (RS) K1, [yon, k2tog] to last st, k1.
Beg with a p row, cont in st st until work measures 21.5 (22.5: 23.5)cm from cast-on edge, ending with RS facing for next row.
FRONT YOKE
Next row (RS) K5, [k2tog, k1] to last 7 sts, k2tog, k5.
71 (75: 79) sts.
K 3 rows.
Beg with a k row, work in st st as follows:
SHAPE ARMHOLES
Cast off 4 sts at beg of next 2 rows. 63 (67: 71) sts.
Dec 1 st at each end of next row and every foll alt row until 51 (55: 59) sts rem.
Cont straight until armhole measures 6 (7.5: 9)cm, ending with RS facing for next row.
DIVIDE FOR NECK
Next row K21 (22: 23) sts, turn and leave rem sts on holder.
P 1 row.
Dec 1 st at neck edge on next row and every foll row until 15 (16: 17) sts rem.
Work straight until armhole measures 10 (11.5: 13)cm, ending with RS facing for next row.
SHAPE SHOULDER
Cast off 5 sts at beg of next row and foll alt row.
5 (6: 7) sts.
Work 1 row.

Cast off rem sts.

With RS facing, slip centre 9 (11: 13) sts onto holder, rejoin yarn to rem sts, k to end of row and complete to match first side of neck, reversing shaping.

LEFT BACK

Cast on 54 (57: 60) sts and work as follows:

Row 1 (RS) [K1, p1] 3 times, k to end of row.

Row 2 P to last 6 sts, [k1, p1] 3 times.

Rep last 2 rows once more.

Next row (picot hem) (RS) K1, [yon, k2tog] to last 1 (0: 1) st, k1 (0: 1).

Next row as row 2.

Next row as row 1.

Next row as row 2.

Rep the last 2 rows until work measures 21.5 (22.5: 23.5)cm from cast-on edge ending RS facing for next row.

BACK YOKE

Next row [K1, p1] 3 times, k13 (16: 19) sts, [k2tog] 15 times, k5. 39 (42: 45) sts.

Work 4 rows in garter stitch with 6-st rib edge, ending with WS facing for next row.

SHAPE ARMHOLE

Next row Cast off 4 sts, p to last 6 sts, [k1, p1] 3 times. 35 (38: 41) sts.

Cont to work in st st with rib edge and shape as follows:

Dec 1 st at armhole edge on next row and every foll alt row until 29 (32: 35) sts rem.

Cont straight until armhole measures 10 (11.5: 13)cm, ending at armhole edge.

SHAPE SHOULDER AND BACK NECK

Cast off 5 sts at beg of next row. 24 (27: 30) sts.

Work 1 row.

Cast off 5 sts, work until there are 8 (9: 10) sts on

right-hand needle, turn and leave rem 11 (13: 15) sts on a holder.

Cast off 3 sts, work to end of row.

Cast off rem 5 (6: 7) sts.

RIGHT BACK

Cast on 54 (57: 60) sts and work as follows:

Row 1 (RS) K to last 6 sts, [p1, k1] 3 times.

Row 2 [P1, k1] 3 times, p to end.

Rep the last 2 rows once more.

Next row (picot hem) (RS) K1, [yon, k2tog] to last 1 (0: 1) st, k1 (0: 1).

Next row as row 2.

Next row as row 1.

Next row as row 2.

Rep the last 2 rows until work measures 21.5 (22.5: 23.5)cm from cast-on edge, ending with RS facing for next row.

FRONT YOKE

Next row (RS) K5, [k2tog] 15 times, k13 (16: 19) sts, [p1, k1] 3 times. 39 (42: 45) sts.

Work 4 rows in garter stitch with 6-st rib edge, ending with RS facing for next row.

SHAPE ARMHOLE

Next row Cast off 4 sts, k to last 6 sts, [p1, k1] 3 times. 35 (38: 41) sts.

P 1 row.

Dec 1 st at armhole edge on next row and every foll alt row until 29 (32: 35) sts rem.

Cont straight until armhole measures 10 (11.5: 13)cm, ending at armhole edge.

SHAPE SHOULDER AND BACK NECK

Cast off 5 sts at beg of next row. 24 (27: 30) sts.

Work 1 row.

Cast off 5 sts, work until there are 8 (9: 10) sts on right-hand needle, turn and leave rem 11 (13: 15) sts

on holder.
Cast off 3 sts, work to end of row.
Cast off rem 5 (6: 7) sts.

SLEEVES

With 2.75mm needles, cast on 38 (42: 46) sts and beg with a k row, work 4 rows in st st.
Next row (picot hem) K1, [yon, k2tog] to last st, k1.
Beg with a p row, cont in st st and inc 1 st at each end of 4th and every foll 6th row until there are 56 (60: 64) sts.
Cont straight until sleeve measures 14.5 (15.5: 16.5)cm from picot row, ending with RS facing for next row.

SHAPE TOP

Cast off 4 sts at beg of next 2 rows. 48 (52: 56) sts.
Work 2 rows straight.
Dec 1 st at each end of next row and foll 4th row, then every foll alt row until 30 (34: 38) sts rem, ending with WS facing for next row.
Next row P7, [p2tog] 8 (10: 12) times, p7. 22 (24: 26) sts.
Cast off.

NECKBAND

Join both shoulder seams.
With RS facing and 2.25mm needles, rejoin yarn and rib as set across first 6 sts from left back holder and k rem 5 (7: 9) sts, then pick up and k3 sts from left back neck edge, 14 sts down left front neck, k9 (11: 13) sts from centre front holder, pick and k14 sts up right front neck, 3 sts along right back neck edge, k first 5 (7: 9) sts from right back holder, then rib rem 6 sts from holder as set. 65 (71: 77) sts.
Work 3 rows in k1, p1 rib as set.
Cast off in rib.

TO FINISH

Weave in any yarn ends.
Gently steam work.
Sew sleeves into armholes, easing to fit.
Join side and sleeve seams.
Turn hems along picot edge and slip stitch into place.
Cut rem linen tape into 4 pieces and attach in pairs to either side of back opening, one pair just at start of neck edging and the other pair at lower edge of yoke.

PANTS

With 2.25mm needles, cast on 52 (56: 60) sts and work in rib as follows:
Row 1 (RS) K2, [p1, k1] to last 2 sts, p2.
Rows 2, 3 and 4 as row 1.
Row 5 (eyelet row) K2, [yf, k2tog, p1, k1] to last 2 sts, yf, k2tog.
Rows 6, 7, 8 and 9 as row 1.
Next row (inc) K6 (6: 7), [inc in next st, k12 (13: 14)] 3 times, inc in next st, k6 (7: 7). 56 (60: 64) sts.
Change to 2.75mm needles.
K 53 (63: 73) rows straight.

DIVIDE FOR LEGS

Row 1 K18 (19: 20) sts, turn and cont on these sts only, leave rem sts on a spare needle.
Row 2 K1, k2tog, k15 (16: 17).
Row 3 K14 (15: 16) sts, k2tog, k1.
Row 4 K1, k2tog, k13 (14: 15) sts.
Cont to dec in this way until 2 sts rem, k2tog.
Fasten off.
With RS facing, rejoin yarn and k across 38 (41: 44) sts on spare needle and work as follows:
Row 1 K15 (16: 17), k2tog, k1, turn and cont on these sts only, leave rem sts on a spare needle.

Row 2 K1, k2tog, knit 14 (15: 16) sts.
Row 3 K13 (14: 15) sts, k2tog, k1.
Row 4 K1, k2tog, k12 (13: 14) sts.
Cont to decrease in this way until 2 sts rem, k2tog.
Fasten off.
With RS facing, rejoin yarn to rem 20 (22: 24) sts and
k 9 (13: 17) rows straight.
Inc 1 st at each end of next row and every foll alt row
until there are 56 (60: 64) sts.
K 71 (81: 93) rows straight.
SHAPE BACK
Rows 1 and 2 K to last 3 sts, turn.
Rows 3 and 4 K to last 6 sts, turn.
Rows 5 and 6 K to last 9 sts, turn.
Rows 7 and 8 K to last 12 sts, turn.
Rows 9 and 10 K to last 15 sts, turn.
Rows 11 and 12 K to last 18 sts, turn.
Rows 13 and 14 K across all sts.
Row 15 K6 (6: 7) [k2tog, k12 (13: 14)] 3 times, k2tog,
k6 (7: 7). 52 (56: 60) sts.
Change to 2.25mm needles.
Row 16 K2, [p1, k1] to last 2 sts, p2.
Rep the last row 3 times more.
Next row (eyelet row) K2, [yf, k2tog, p1, k1] to last 2
sts, yf, k2tog.
Next row K2, [p1, k1] to last 2 sts, p2.
Rep the last row, 3 times more.
Cast off in rib.

TO FINISH
Join side seams.
Cut approximately 80cm of linen tape, thread
through the eyelets and tie in a bow at the front.

RECYCLED RAG BASKET

see pages 46–47

Strips of fabric from favourite discarded or worn clothes, or bargain remnants of cloth are washed and cut and knitted into a basic cross-shape that assembles into a simple basket. Knitted in moss/seed stitch they make a special piece for the nursery to keep essential creams and lotions to hand or to store little vests and bits and bobs.

SIZE
Small 16cm wide x 16cm long x 16cm high
Large 20cm wide x 29cm long x 12cm high

MATERIALS
Lengths of linens in various colours – approximately 0.5m cut into 1.5cm wide strips and rolled into balls – these baskets were made from a mixture of natural linens, pale and dark lavender colour linen, brown gingham linen and a tea towel stripe
Pair of 6.5mm knitting needles
Large-eyed blunt-tipped sewing needle

TIPS AND TECHNIQUES
* Instructions for the large basket are given in round brackets.
* When changing to another fabric, hold two ends together and work the next stitch, rather than knotting the two ends, which can look rather lumpy.
* Weave any long ends into the fabric when you have finished knitting.

TO MAKE SMALL (LARGE) BASKET
Cast on 11 (15) sts and work 16 (12)cm in moss st.
Cast on 12 (9) sts at beg of next 2 rows. 35 (33) sts.
Cont straight in moss st for a further 15(29)cm.
Cast off 12 (9) sts at the beg of the next 2 rows.
11 (15) sts.
Cont straight in moss st for a further 16 (12)cm on these sts.
Cast off in moss st.

TO FINISH
Weave in any yarn ends.
Lay work out flat and fold each corner up in turn.
Over sew each corner in turn with a strip of fabric.
For added rigidity, if required, over-sew all around top edge.

SWEATER AND TROUSERS

see pages 48–49

Basic pieces knitted in pure organic cotton for ultimate comfort. Pair the simplest long sleeve sweater – featuring a button shoulder, ticket pocket and rolled edges – with easy 'pull-on' trousers – complete with roll-edge cuffs and back pocket detail.

SIZES
To fit 0–3(3–6: 6–9) months

MATERIALS
Sweater 3 (4: 4) x 50g balls of double knitting-weight organic cotton, such as Rowan Purelife Organic Cotton Naturally Dyed DK in blue
Trousers 3 (3: 4) x 50g balls of double knitting-weight organic cotton, such as Rowan Purelife Organic Cotton Naturally Dyed DK in green
Pair each of 3.25mm and 3.75 mm knitting needles
2 x 1.5cm diameter horn buttons for sweater
Waist length of 2cm wide elastic for trousers

TENSION
22 sts and 30 rows to 10cm square over st st using 3.75mm needles. Always work a tension swatch and change needles accordingly if necessary.

ABBREVIATIONS
See page 139.

TIPS AND TECHNIQUES
Fully fashioned increase
K3, m1, k to last 3 sts, m1, k3.
Fully fashioned decrease
K3, k2tog, k to last 5 sts, k2tog tbl, k3.

SWEATER

BACK
Using 3.25mm needles, cast on 60 (64: 68) sts and beg with a k row, work 6 rows in st st.
Change to 3.75mm needles and cont straight in st st until work measures 14.5 (16.5: 18.5)cm from cast-on edge ending with RS facing for next row.
SHAPE ARMHOLES
Cast off 3 sts at beg of next 2 rows. 54 (58: 62) sts.
Dec 1 st at each end of next row and 3 foll alt rows. 46 (50: 54) sts.
Cont straight until armhole measure 10 (11: 12)cm ending with RS facing for next row.
SHAPE BACK NECK AND SHOULDERS
Next row K15 (16: 18) sts, turn.
Next row Cast off 2 sts, p to end of row.
Work 2 rows straight.
Cast off rem 13 (14: 16) sts.
With RS facing, slip centre 16 (18: 18) sts onto holder, rejoin yarn to rem sts and k to end of row.
Next row P.
Next row Cast off 2 sts, k to end of row. 13 (14: 16) sts.
Next row P.
Change to 3.25mm needles and work in rib as follows:
Next row [K1, p1] to last 1 (0: 0) st, k1 (0: 0).
Next row P1 (0: 0), [k1, p1] to end.
Rep these 2 rows twice more.
Cast off in rib.

POCKET (MAKE ONE)
Using 3.75mm needles, cast on 8 (10: 12) sts and beg with a k row, work 2 rows in st st.
Inc 1 st at each end of next row and 2 foll alt rows. 14 (16: 18) sts.

Work straight until pocket measures 6 (7: 8)cm, ending with WS facing for next row.
Change to 3.25mm needles and work 2 rows in st st.
Cast off purlwise.

FRONT
Work as Back until armhole measures 7 (8: 9)cm, ending with RS facing for next row.

Next row K19 (20: 22) sts, turn.
Next row Cast off 3 sts, p to end of row.
Work 1 row straight.
Dec 1 st at neck edge on every row until 13 (14: 16) sts rem.
Work straight until armhole measures 10 (11: 12)cm ending with RS facing for next row.
Change to 3.25mm needles and work in rib as follows:
Next row (RS) [K1, p1] to last 1 (0: 0) st, k1 (0: 0).
Next row P1 (0: 0), [k1, p1] to end.
Next row (buttonhole row) Rib 3, yf, k2tog, rib 3 (4: 6) sts, yf, work 2tog, rib 3.
Work 3 more rows in rib.
Cast off in rib.
With RS facing, slip 8 (10: 10) sts at centre front onto a holder, rejoin yarn to rem sts , cast off 3 sts, k to end.
Next row Cast off 3 sts, work to end.
P 1 row.
Dec 1 st at neck edge on every row until 13 (14: 16) sts rem.
Work straight in st st until armhole measures 11 (12: 13)cm.
Cast off.

SLEEVES
Using 3.25mm needles, cast on 38 (40: 42) sts and beg with a k row, work 6 rows in st st.

Change to 3.75mm needles, cont in st st and inc 1 st at each end of 3rd and every foll 6th row until 50 (54: 58) sts.
Work straight until sleeve measures 14.5 (16.5: 19.5)cm from cast-on edge, ending with RS facing for next row.

Cast off 3 sts at beg of next 4 (4: 6) rows. 38 (42: 40) sts.
Cast off 2 sts at beg of next 4 (6: 2) rows. 30 (30: 36) sts.
Cast off 3 sts at beg of next 4 (2: 4) rows. 18 (24: 24) sts.
Cast off 4 sts at beg of next 2 rows. 10 (16: 16) sts.
Cast off.

NECKBAND
Join right shoulder seam.
With RS facing and 3.25mm needles, pick up and k13 (14: 16) sts along rib and down left front neck, k across 8 (10: 10) sts from centre front holder, pick up and k13 (14: 16) sts up right front neck, 3 sts down right back neck, k across 16 (18: 18) sts from centre back holder, then pick up and k8 sts from left back neck and along rib. 61 (67: 71) sts.
Beg with a p row, work 7 rows in st st.
Cast off.

TO FINISH
Weave in any yarn ends.
Lay work out flat and gently steam
Place buttonhole band over button band and slip stitch edges together along armhole edge.
Sew sleeves into armholes easing to fit.
Join side and sleeve seams. Sew on buttons.
Sew on pocket approximately 10 (11: 12)cm down from shoulder and 5cm in from side seam.

TROUSERS

RIGHT LEG

Using 3.75 mm needles cast on 52 (54: 56) sts and beg with a k row, work 7 rows in st st, ending with WS facing for next row.

Ridge row (WS) K.

Beg with a k row, work 8 rows in st st.

SHAPE BACK

Row 1 K10 (11: 12) sts, turn.
Row 2 P to end.
Row 3 K21 (22: 23) sts, turn.
Row 4 P to end.
Row 5 K32 (33: 34) sts, turn.
Row 6 P to end.
Row 7 K43 (44: 45) sts, turn.
Row 8 P to end.

Cont straight across all 52 (54: 56) sts for a further 16 (18: 22) rows.

Inc 1 st (see note on fully fashioned inc) at each end of next row and every foll 6th row until there are 62 (64: 66) sts.

Work 3 rows straight.

Cast on 4 sts at beg of next 2 rows. 70 (72: 74) sts.

SHAPE LEG

Dec 1 st (see note on fully fashioned dec) at each end of 5th and every foll 6th row until 60 (62: 64) sts rem.

Cont straight for 3 (9: 15) rows, ending with RS facing for next row.

Change to 3.25mm needles and work 6 rows in st st. Cast off.

LEFT LEG

Using 3.75 mm needles, cast on 52 (54: 56) sts and beg with a k row, work 7 rows in st st, ending with WS facing for next row.

Ridge row (WS) K.

Beg with a k row, work 9 rows in st st.

SHAPE BACK

Row 1 P10 (11: 12) sts, turn.
Row 2 K to end.
Row 3 P21 (22: 23) sts, turn.
Row 4 K to end.
Row 5 P32 (33: 34) sts, turn.
Row 6 K to end.
Row 7 P43 (44: 45) sts, turn.
Row 8 K to end.

Cont straight across all 52 (54: 56) sts for a further 15 (17: 21) rows.

Inc 1 st (see note on fully fashioned inc) at each end of next row and every foll 6th row until there are 62 (64: 66) sts.

Work 3 rows straight.

Cast on 4 sts at beg of next 2 rows. 70 (72: 74) sts.

SHAPE LEG

Dec 1 st (see note on fully fashioned dec) at each end of 5th and every foll 6th row until 60 (62: 64) sts rem.

Cont straight for 3 (9: 15) rows, ending with RS facing for next row.

Change to 3.25mm needles and work 6 rows in st st. Cast off.

POCKET (MAKE ONE)

Work exactly as for Sweater pocket.

TO FINISH

Weave in any yarn ends. Lay work out flat and gently steam.Join back and front seams. Join leg seam, reversing seam at lower edge, to allow hems to roll. Turn waistband to inside along ridge row and slip stitch in place, leaving a gap. Insert elastic, join ends and close gap in seam.Sew on pocket.

BOOTEES AND BONNET

see pages 52–55

Pretty, dainty shoes knitted in a lacy pattern with contrast garter stitch soles and uppers and fastened with a tiny natural mother of pearl button. The hat is a simple pull-on design worked in garter stitch and edged with the same lacy pattern as the Mary Jane-style bootees, and a shell edging. Both are made in fine milk cotton yarn.

SIZES
To fit 0–3 (3–6: 6–9) months
Length of bootees 8 (9: 10)cm

MATERIALS
1 x 50g ball of 4ply-weight milk cotton, such as Rowan Fine Milk Cotton 4 ply in pink or white
Pair of 2.75mm knitting needles
2 small mother of pearl buttons for shoes and 1 button for flower

TENSION
30 sts and 38 rows to 10cm square over st st using 2.75mm needles. Always work a tension swatch and change needles accordingly if necessary.

ABBREVIATIONS
See page 139.

BOOTEES

LEFT UPPER
Using yarn held double, cast on 50 (58: 66) sts.
Cut one strand of yarn and using a single strand of yarn, k 3 rows.
Next row K1, * p1, yon (to make a st), k1; rep from * to last st, k1. 74 (86: 98) sts.
Next row K1, * p1, yon, k2tog; rep from * to last st, k1.
Rep the last row 2 (4: 4) times more.
Next row K2, * p1, k2tog; rep from * to end of row. 50 (58: 66) sts.
Cont in garter st and work as follows:
Next row K20 (24: 28), k2tog, k6, k2tog, k20 (24: 28). 48 (56: 64) sts.
Next row K19 (23: 27), k2tog, k6, k2tog, k19 (23: 27). 46 (54: 62) sts.
Next row K18 (22: 26), k2tog, k6, k2tog, k18 (22: 26). 44 (52: 60) sts.
Next row K17 (21: 25), k2tog, k6, k2tog, k17 (21: 25). 42 (50: 58) sts.
Next row K16 (20: 24), k2tog, k6, k2tog, k16 (20: 24). 40 (48: 56) sts.
Next row K15 (19: 23), k2tog, k6, k2tog, k15 (19: 23). 38 (46: 54) sts.
Next row K14 (18: 22), k2tog, k6, k2tog, k14 (18: 22). 36 (44: 52) sts. **
Next row K10 (12: 14) sts, turn and k 3 rows.
Cast off.
Rejoin yarn to rem sts, cast off centre 16 (20: 24) sts, cast on 12 (14: 16) sts, k to end of row. 22 (26: 30) sts.
Buttonhole row K to last 3 sts, yf, k2tog, k1.
K 2 rows.
Cast off.

RIGHT UPPER

Work as Left Upper to **.

Next row K10 (12: 14) sts, turn, leaving rem 26 (32: 38) sts on a spare needle and cast on 12 (14: 16) sts. 22 (26: 30) sts.

K 1 row.

Buttonhole row K to last 3 sts, yf, k2tog, k1.

K 2 rows.

Cast off.

Rejoin yarn to rem sts, cast off centre 16 (20: 24) sts, k to end of row.

K 3 rows.

Cast off.

SOLES (MAKE TWO)

Using yarn double throughout, cast on 8 sts.

K 4 rows.

Next row K and inc 1 st at each end of row. 10 sts.

K 4 (6: 8) rows.

Next row K and dec 1 st at each end of row. 8 sts.

K 6 (7: 8) rows.

Next row K and inc 1 st at each end of row. 10 sts.

K 4 (6: 8) rows.

Next row: K and inc 1 st at each end of row. 12 sts.

K 4 rows.

K and dec 1 st at each end of next 3 rows. 6 sts.

Cast off.

TO FINISH

Join heel seam.

Sew sole to upper.

Sew on buttons.

BONNET

Using 2.75mm needles, cast on 97 (112: 127) sts and work as follows:

Row 1 (RS) K1, yo, * k5, slip the 2nd, 3rd, 4th and 5th sts over the first st, yo; rep from * to last st, k1.

Row 2 P1, * [p1, yon, k1 tbl] all into next st, p1; rep from * to end. 81 (93: 105) sts.

Row 3 K and dec 1 st at end of row. 80 (92: 104) sts.

Rows 4, 5 and 6 K1, * p1, yon, k2tog; rep from * to last st, k1.

Row 7 K and inc 1(dec 1: dec 3) sts evenly across row. 81 (91: 101) sts.

Cont in garter st until hat measures 8.5 (10: 11.5)cm from cast-on edge.

SHAPE TOP

Cont in garter stitch and shape top as follows:

Next row K1, [k2tog, k8] to end of row. 73 (82: 91) sts.

K 3 rows.

Next row K1, [k2tog, k7] to end of row. 65 (73: 81) sts.

K 3 rows.

Next row K1, [k2tog, k6] to end of row. 57 (64: 71) sts.

K 3 rows.

Next row K1, [k2tog, k5] to end of row. 49 (55: 61) sts.

K 3 rows.

Next row K1, [k2tog, k4] to end of row. 41 (46: 51) sts.

K 1 row.

Next row K1, [k2tog, k3] to end of row. 33 (37: 41) sts.

Work 1 row straight.

Next row K1, [k2tog, k2] to end of row. 25 (28: 31) sts.

Work 1 row straight
Next row K1, [k2tog, k1] to end of row.
17 (19: 21) sts.
Next row K1, [k2tog] to end of row. 9 (10: 11) sts.
Cut yarn leaving long end, thread through rem sts,
pull up and secure.
Fasten off and join seam.

LACE FLOWER
Using 2.75mm needles, cast on 49 sts.
Row 1 (WS) P.
Row 2 K1, * yon, k1, sl 1, k2tog, psso, k1, yon, k1; rep
from * to end of row.
Rep last 2 rows twice more.
Next row P.
Next row [P2tog] to last st, p1. 25 sts.
Next row [K2tog] to last st, k1. 13 sts.
Cut yarn, thread through rem sts, pull up tight and
fasten securely.

TO FINISH
Attach flower securely to hat.

LACE CUSHION

see pages 56–57

Pretty yet simple cushion cover knitted in a collection of lace stitch, eyelets and moss stitch for texture. The back is worked in basic stocking stitch and the lacy edged is softly gathered and the cushion is finished with natural cotton ties.

SIZE
40cm x 30cm

MATERIALS
4 x 50g balls of double knitting-weight cashmere-cotton blend, such as Lanaknits Cashmere Canapa DK in ecru
Pair of 3.75mm knitting needles
40cm x 30cm feather cushion pad
1.5m of 1cm wide cotton tape for ties

TENSION
22 sts and 34 rows to 10cm square over st st using 3.75mm needles. Always work a tension swatch and change needles accordingly if necessary.

ABBREVIATIONS
See page 139.

TIPS AND TECHNIQUES
* The back of the cushion is worked in st st with a single rib selvedge edge to one side.

CUSHION FRONT
Cast on 87 sts and work in moss st and lace pattern as follows:
Row 1 K1, [p1, k1] 28 times, k5, p2, k9, yf, k1, yf, k3, sl 1, k2tog, psso, p2, k5.
Row 2 and every foll WS row P30, [k1, p1] 28 times, k1.
Row 3 K1, [p1, k1] 28 times, k5, p2, k10, yf, k1, yf, k2, sl1, k2tog, psso, p2, k5.
Row 5 (eyelet row) K1, [p1, k1] 28 times, k2, yo, k2tog, k1, p2, k3tog, k4, yf, k1, yf, k3, [yf, k1] twice, sl1, k2tog, psso, p2, k2, yo, k2tog, k1.
Row 7 K1, [p1, k1] 28 times, k5, p2, k3tog, k3, yf, k1, yf, k9, p2, k5.
Row 9 K1, [p1, k1] 28 times, k5, p2, k3tog, k2, yf, k1, yf, k10, p2, k5.
Row 11 (eyelet row) K1, [p1, k1] 28 times, k2, yo, k2tog, k1, p2, k3tog, [k1, yf] twice, k3, yf, k1, yf, k4, sl 1, k2tog, psso, p2, k2, yo, k2tog, k1.
Row 12 P30, [k1, p1] 28 times, k1.
Rep last 12 rows until work measures 30cm from cast-on edge, ending with RS facing for next row.
Cast off.

CUSHION BACK
Cast on 87 sts and work as follows:
Row 1 [K1, p1] 3 times, k to end of row.
Row 2 P to last 6 sts, [k1, p1] 3 times.
Rep last 2 rows until work measures 30cm from cast-on edge, ending with RS facing for next row.
Cast off.

DOUBLE DIAMOND LACE EDGING
Cast on 9 sts.
Row 1 and every alternate row (RS) K.
Row 2 K3, k2tog, yf, k2tog, [yf, k1] twice. 10 sts.

Row 4 K2, [k2tog, yf] twice, k3, yf, k1. 11 sts.
Row 6 K1, [k2tog, yf] twice, k5, yf, k1. 12 sts.
Row 8 K3, [yf, k2tog] twice, k1, k2tog, yf, k2tog.
11 sts.
Row 10 K4, yf, k2tog, yf, k3tog, yf, k2tog. 10 sts.
Row 12 K5, yf, k3tog, yf, k2tog. 9 sts.
Rep these 12 rows until edging measures 160cm,
ending with RS facing for next row.
Cast off.
Join cast-on and cast-off edges.

TO MAKE UP
Weave in any yarn ends.
Lay pieces flat and gently steam work.
With WS of work facing, place cushion front with
lace panel to the left, over cushion back with rib edge
to the left. Join three sides, leaving lace and rib end
open. Turn through to right side.
Attach edging along seam line and open edge, slightly
gathering as you work, and pinching more fully in
each corner.
Cut cotton tape into four pieces and attach in pairs
to each side of cushion opening.
Insert pad and tie tapes.

BIRD MOBILE

see pages 60–63

A pretty play on a traditional pram toy, with knitted silhouette birds and covered knitted beads. These are assembled with shiny natural buttons, wooden beads and silk ribbons to create a simple and inexpensive toy, or mobile.

MATERIALS

FOR MOBILE:

1 x 50g ball of double knitting-weight organic cotton, such as Rowan Purelife Organic Cotton Naturally Dyed DK in each of pink and mid blue

Pair of 3.75mm knitting needles

1 x 35mm wooden bead

2 x 20mm wooden beads

1m of 7mm wide silk ribbon in each of pale green and pale pink

1 x 15mm diameter mother of pearl button

Approximately 5m of hemp yarn

Wire coathanger

FOR PRAM TOY:

1 x 50g ball of 4ply-weight milk cotton yarn, such as Rowan Fine Milk Cotton in each of pink, barley sugar, lilac, liquorice and turquoise

Pair of 2.25mm knitting needles

5 x 30mm wooden beads

8 x 20mm wooden beads

1m of 7mm wide silk ribbon in each of pale peach, turquoise and lavender

3 x 25mm diameter mother of pearl buttons

Approximately 1m of hemp yarn

FOR BOTH PROJECTS

Natural organic cotton stuffing

Large-eyed blunt tipped sewing needle

Templates for the wings (see page 135)

Scraps of cotton and linen fabrics

Embroidery thread

TIPS AND TECHNIQUES

* The birds and wooden bead covers for the mobile and pram toy are worked from the same instructions, using the yarn and needles as specified above.

* Increases are worked as kfb (knit into front and back of next st).

TO MAKE BIRD

(make 4 for pram toy and 1 for mobile)

Cast on 8 sts.

Beg with a k row, work 14 rows in st st.

Row 15 K and inc 1 st at each end of row. 10 sts.

Beg with a p row, work 9 rows in st st.

Row 25 Kfb, k2, m1, k4, m1, k1, kfb, k1. 14 sts.

Row 26 P.

Row 27 Kfb, k3, m1, k6, m1, k2, kfb, k1. 18 sts.

Row 28 P.

Row 29 Kfb, k4, m1, k8, m1, k3, kfb, k1. 22 sts.

Row 30 P.

Row 31 Kfb, k5, m1, k10, m1, k4, kfb, k1. 26 sts.

Beg with a p row, work 5 rows in st st.

Row 37 K2tog tbl, k to last 2 sts, k2tog. 24 sts.

Row 38 P.

Row 39 K2tog tbl, k4, k2tog, k8, k2tog tbl, k4, k2tog. 20 sts.

Row 40 P.

Row 41 K2tog tbl, k3, k2tog, k6, k2tog tbl, k3, k2tog. 16 sts.

Beg with a p row, work 5 rows in st st.

Row 47 K2tog tbl, k to last 2 sts, k2tog. 14 sts.

Row 48 P.

Row 49 K2tog tbl, k to last 2 sts, k2tog. 12 sts.

Row 50 P.
Row 51 K2tog tbl, k2, k2tog, k2tog tbl, k2, k2tog.
8 sts.
Row 52 [P2tog] to end of row. 4 sts.
Row 53 K1, k2tog, k1. 3 sts.
Row 54 Sl1, p2tog, psso.
Fasten off.
Fold in half and join seam, stuffing as you go.

TO COVER WOODEN BEAD
(make 5 for pram toy and 1 for mobile)
Cast on 11 sts.
Row 1 [Kfb] to end. 22 sts.
Beg with a p row, work 11 rows in st st.
Row 13 [K2tog] to end of row. 11 sts.
Row 14 [P2tog] to last st, p1. 6 sts.
Cut yarn leaving a long end, thread through sts, pull
up tightly and secure firmly. Do not cut yarn, but use
it to join side seam, insert wooden bead and gather
up cast on edge around bead. Fasten off securely.

TO ASSEMBLE THE PRAM TOY
Take approx 1m of hemp yarn, make a loop at one
end by tying a slip knot, pass 2 x 20mm wooden
beads over the end, * thread on a covered bead, a
button and 1 x 20mm wooden bead; rep from * once,
** thread on a covered bead, 1 x 20mm wooden bead
and a button; rep from ** once, thread on a covered
bead, add 2 x 20mm wooden beads, then spacing all
the elements out so that the final length will be
approximately 55cm, tie a slip knot in end of string.
Using the wing templates on page 135, cut one wing
in fabric for each bird and stitch onto the side of the
birds, then on the other side, embroider French knots
or small flowers to decorate.
Take ribbon lengths and tie around birds, criss-

crossing body and attach to main string and tie in a
secure bow, adjusting height away from baby.

TO ASSEMBLE THE MOBILE
Bend the wire coathanger into a circle. Completely
wrap the wire in narrow lengths of assorted fabrics
and bind the hook of the hanger in hemp yarn.
Tie small pieces of fabric over the wrapping, then tie
a ribbon bow at the base of the hook and another at
the bottom of the circle.
Using the wing templates on page 135, cut 2 wing
pieces from fabric and sew to each side of bird and
decorate with French knots.
Tie the bird to one end of a length of hemp yarn,
thread on a 15mm wooden bead, a button, a covered
wooden bead, held on place with knots, and another
15mm wooden bead, tie a knot to hold in place, then
tie to the base of the hook to hang in the centre of
the circle.

SOAKER PANTS

see pages 64–65

A traditional knitted garment for baby, which is back in vogue amongst today's environmentally concerned new mothers, these soaker pants are a simple nappy cover for both day- and night-time. Knitted in an organic cotton, which is naturally antibacterial and breathable, this yarn comes in many pretty shades that are created from herb and plant dyes. The purest yarn for the softest skin.

SIZE
To fit 0–3(3–6: 6–9) months

MATERIALS
2 (2: 2) x 50g balls of double knitting-weight organic cotton, such as Rowan Purelife Organic Cotton Naturally Dyed DK in pink, green or ecru
Pair each of 3mm and 3.75mm knitting needles
Waist length of 2cm wide soft elastic
25cm of 1.5cm cotton tape (optional)

TENSION
22 sts and 30 rows to 10cm square over st st using 3.75mm needles. Always work a tension swatch and change needles accordingly if necessary.

ABBREVIATIONS
See page 139.

BACK
* Using 3.75mm needles, cast on 19 sts.
SHAPE LEGS AND CROTCH
Row 1 K.
Row 2 Cast on 6 sts and p all sts.
Row 3 Cast on 6 sts and k these 6 sts, skpo, k15, k2tog, k to end.
Row 4 Cast on 6 sts and p all sts.
Row 5 Cast on 6 sts and k these 6 sts, k6, skpo, k13, k2tog, k to end.
Row 6 Cast on 9 sts and p all sts.
Row 7 Cast on 9 sts, k these 9 sts, k12, skpo, k11, k2tog, k to end.
Row 8 Cast on 9 sts and p all sts.
Row 9 Cast on 9 sts, k these 9 sts, k21, skpo, k9, k2tog, k to end.
Row 10 Cast on 2 (3: 4) sts and p all sts.
Row 11 Cast on 2 (3: 4) sts, k these 2 (3: 4) sts, k30, skpo, k7, k2tog, k to end. 73 (75: 77) sts.
Row 12 P.
Place a marker at each end of last row.
Row 13 K32 (33: 34) sts, skpo, k5, k2tog, k to end.
Row 14 P.
Row 15 K32 (33: 34) sts, skpo, k3, k2tog, k to end.
Row 16 P.
Row 17 K32 (33: 34) sts, skpo, k1, k2tog, k to end.
Row 18 P.
Row 19 K32 (33: 34) sts, sl 1, k2tog, psso, k to end. 65 (67: 69) sts.
Row 20 P.
Cont straight in st st until work measures 12.5 (13.5: 14.5)cm from markers ending with RS facing for next row. *
SHAPE BACK
Row 1 K56 (58: 60) sts, turn.
Row 2 P47 (49: 51) sts, turn.

Row 3 K37 (39: 41) sts, turn.
Row 4 P27 (29: 31) sts, turn.
Row 5 K17 (19: 21) sts, turn.
Row 6 P7 (9: 11) sts, turn.
Row 7 K all sts.
Row 8 P all sts.
** Change to 3mm needles and work waistband as follows:
Work 8 rows in st st, ending with RS facing for next row.
Next row P to make turning ridge.
Beg with a p row, work 7 rows in st st, ending with RS facing for next row.
Cast off all sts loosely. **

FRONT
Work as Back from * to * and then as Back from ** to **.

TO MAKE UP
Weave in any yarn ends.
Gently steam work.
Join crotch seam using mattress stitch.

LEG BANDS
With RS facing and 3mm needles, pick up and k64 (66: 68) sts evenly around leg shaping and work 5 rows in k1, p1 rib.
Cast off in rib.
Rep for other leg.

TO FINISH.
Join side seams.
Turn waistband to inside along ridge row and slip stitch into place, leaving gap. Insert elastic, sew ends. Close gap.

Optional – Make a bow from cotton tape and sew to front of pants.

HEIRLOOM COT COVER

see pages 66–67

Treasured pieces of vintage fabric are a constant source of inspiration. Combined with squares of knitted lace worked in a cashmere-hemp yarn, the simple embroidered cottons of yesteryear create an especially pretty and covetable cot cover. Once assembled, the squares are backed with broderie anglaise and edged in old lace. Keeping the colours within the design neutral makes it easier to collate the fabric pieces, giving it timeless appeal.

SIZE
Approximately 100cm x 80cm (excluding edging)

MATERIALS
4 x 50g balls of double knitting-weight cashmere-cotton blend, such as Lanaknits Cashmere Canapa DK in ecru
Pair of 4mm knitting needles
10 x 23cm squares of vintage (or similar) fabric
Lightweight iron-on interfacing
Approximately 7m of narrow lace
Microfilament
Approximately 3.8m of edging lace
Approximately 110cm x 90cm piece of sheeting (to mount the cover)
Approximately 110cm x 90cm piece of broderie anglaise (or similar) for backing the cover

TENSION
22 sts and 28 rows to 10cm square over st st using 4mm needles. Always work a tension swatch and change needles accordingly if necessary.

ABBREVIATIONS
See page 139.

TIPS AND TECHNIQUES
* For neat edges, slip the first st and work into the back of the last st on every row of every square.

DIAMOND LACE (MAKE TWO)
Cast on 39 sts.
P 1 row.
Row 1 (RS) * K4, yf, skpo; rep from * to last 3 sts, k3.
Row 2 and every WS row Purl.
Row 3 K2, * k2tog, yf, k1, yf, skpo, k1; rep from * to last st, k1.
Row 5 K1, k2tog, yf, * k3, yf, sl 1, k2tog, psso, yf; rep from * to last 6 sts, k3, yf, skpo, k1.
Row 7 K3, * yf, sl 1, k2tog, psso, yf, k3; rep from * to end of row.
Row 9 As Row 1.
Row 11 K1, * yf, skpo, k4; rep from * to last 2 sts, yf, skpo.
Row 13 K2, * yf, skpo, k1, k2tog, yf, k1; rep from * to last st, k1.
Row 15 As row 7.
Row 17 As row 5.
Row 19 As row 11.
Row 20 Purl.
The last 20 rows form the pattern and are repeated.
Work 50 rows, so ending with the 10th row of 3rd repeat.
K 1 row.
Cast off.

LACY CHECKS (MAKE TWO)

Cast on 41 sts.

P 1 row.

Row 1 (RS) K1, * yf, sl 1, k2tog, psso, yf, k3; rep from * to last 4 sts, yf, sl 1, k2tog, psso, yf, k1.

Row 2 and every WS row Purl.

Row 3 As row 1.

Row 5 Knit.

Row 7 K4, * yf, sl 1, k2tog, psso, yf, k3; rep from * to last st, k1.

Row 9 As row 7.

Row 11 Knit.

Row 12 Purl.

The last 12 rows form the pattern and are repeated.

Work 48 rows, so ending with the 12th row of 4th repeat.

Cast off.

STAGGERED FERN LACE PANEL (MAKE TWO)

Cast on 44 sts.

P 1 row.

Row 1 (RS) K2, * p2, k9, yf, k1, yf, k3, sl 1, k2tog, psso, p2; rep from * once more, k2.

Row 2 and every WS row Purl.

Row 3 K2, * p2, k10, yf, k1, yf, k2, sl 1, k2tog, psso, p2; rep from * once more, k2.

Row 5 K2, * p2, k3tog, k4, yf, k1, yf, k3, [yf, k1] twice, sl 1, k2tog, psso, p2; rep from * once more, k2.

Row 7 K2, * p2, k3tog, k3, yf, k1, yf, k9, p2; rep from * once more, k2.

Row 9 K2, * p2, k3tog, k2, yf, k1, yf, k10, p2; rep from * once more, k2.

Row 11 K2, * p2, k3tog, [k1, yf] twice, k3, yf, k1, yf, k4, sl 1, k2tog, psso, p2; rep from * once more, k2.

Row 12 Purl.

The last 12 rows form the pattern and are repeated.

Work 48 rows, so ending with the 12th row of 4th repeat.

K 1 row.

Cast off.

ZIG ZAG EYELETS (MAKE TWO)

Cast on 45 sts.

P 1 row.

Row 1 (RS) K4, * yf, skpo, k5; rep from * to last 6 sts, yf, skpo, k4.

Row 2 and every WS row Purl.

Row 3 K5, * yf, skpo, k5; rep from * to last 5 sts, yf, skpo, k3.

Row 5 K6, * yf, skpo, k5; rep from * to last 4 sts, yf, skpo, k2.

Row 7 K7, * yf, skpo, k5; rep from * to last 3 sts, yf, skpo, k1.

Row 9 K3, * k2tog, yf, k5; rep from * to last 7 sts, k2tog, yf, k5.

Row 11 K2, * k2tog, yf, k5; rep from * to last 8 sts, k2tog, yf, k6.

Row 13 K1, * k2tog, yf, k5; rep from * to last 9 sts, k2tog, yf, k7.

Row 15 * K2tog, yf, k5; rep from * to last 10 sts, k2tog, yf, k8.

Row 16 Purl.

The last 16 rows form the pattern and are repeated.

Work 48 rows, so ending with the 16th row of 3rd repeat.

K 1 row.

Cast off.

LACE DIAMOND BORDER (MAKE TWO)

Cast on 40 sts.

P 1 row.

Row 1 (RS) * K1, yf, k3, pass 3rd st on right hand needle over first 2 sts; rep from * to end of row.

Row 2 and every WS row Purl.
Row 3 Knit.
Row 5 K3, * yf, skpo, k6; rep from * to last 6 sts, yf, skpo, k3.
Row 7 K2, * [yf, skpo] twice, k4; rep from * to last 7 sts, [yf, skpo] twice, k2.
Row 9 K1, * [yf, skpo] 3 times, k2; rep from * to last 8 sts, [yf, skpo,] 3 times, k1.
Row 11 As row 7.
Row 13 As row 5.
Row 15 Knit.
Row 16 Purl.
The last 16 rows form the pattern and are repeated.
Work 52 rows, so ending with the 4th row of 4th repeat.
Cast off.

TO MAKE UP
Each knitted piece should measure 20cm square, gently press each piece, easing to shape and size.
Iron interfacing onto the wrong side of each fabric square and lightly mark out the centre 20cm square.
The cot cover is made up of 5 lines of 4 squares.
Arrange the knitted and fabric squares to create a good mix, the knitted squares can be placed horizontally, vertically or reversed.
Sewing the knitted pieces directly onto the fabric pieces, using the marked 20cm outlines on the fabrics as a guide, make the 5 strips of 4 squares.
Sew the 5 strips together, to create the cover and gently press.
Lay the cover onto the sheeting and sew around the edge, easing the knitted pieces into place to avoid stretching.
Using microfilament and a zig-zag stitch, sew narrow lace over the edges of the squares to hide the seams.

The fancy edge of the lace should face the fabric pieces, so will need to be twisted at the corners (see diagram opposite).
With the straight edge of the lace edging aligned with the edge of the cover and with extra fullness at the corners, machine stitch the lace to the right side of the cover so the fancy edge faces inward.
Press the lace so the fancy edge faces outward and hand sew the join of the lace.
With wrong sides facing, lay the cover onto the broderie anglaise backing piece and fold in the hem allowances all around the edge. Hand sew the cover to the backing. Press gently.

SPOTTY GIRAFFE

see pages 68–69

A quirky knitted giraffe toy. Worked in organic cotton and embroidered with spots in a contrast colour, the added suede ears and tail give this giraffe his unique character.

SIZE
Approximately 32cm high

MATERIALS
2 x 50g balls of double knitting-weight cotton, such as Rowan Handknit Cotton DK in ecru (A) and 1 x 50g ball of lilac (B) and oddments in taupe (C)
Pair of 3.75mm knitting needles
Natural organic cotton stuffing
Scrap of suede or felt
2 small buttons
50cm of 15mm wide tape or ribbon
Templates for the ears and tail (see page 135)

TENSION
22 sts and 40 rows to 10cm square over patt using 3.75mm needles. Always work a tension swatch and change needles accordingly if necessary.

ABBREVIATIONS
See page 139.

TIPS AND TECHNIQUES
* Giraffe is worked throughout in st st using 3.75mm needles.

BODY AND LEGS
* Starting with back leg and C, cast on 14 sts and work 2 rows in st st.
Next row K2tog, k to last 2 sts, k2tog. 12 sts.
Work 4 rows.
Change to A.
Beg with a p row, work 9 rows.
Next row K1, m1, k to last st, m1, k1. 14 sts.
Rep the last 10 rows twice more. 18 sts.
Beg with a p row, work 3 rows. *
Leave on a spare needle.
Rep from * to * for second leg.
Next row (RS) K18 from second leg, then k across 18 sts from first leg. 36 sts.
Work 2 rows.
Next row P17 sts, m1, p2, m1, p17.
Next row K16, m1, k6, m1, k16.
Next row P15, m1, p10, m1, p15.
Cont in this way to inc 2 sts on every row, working 4 sts more between incs until there are 60 sts.
Next row P7, p2tog, p42, p2tog, p7.
Next row K8, k2tog, k38, k2tog, k8.
Cont in this way to dec 2 sts on every row, working 1 st more before first dec and after second dec and 4 sts less between the decs until 40 sts rem.
Beg with a p row, work 16 rows.
Next row P2tog, p to last 2 sts, p2tog.
Beg with a k row, work 13 rows.
Next row P2tog, p to last 2 sts, p2tog. 36 sts.
Now divide for the front legs
Next row K18, turn, leave rem 18 sts on a holder.
** Beg with a p row, work 10 rows
Next row P2tog, p to last 2 sts, p2tog.
Beg with a k row, work 7 rows.
Rep last 8 rows twice more.
Work 11 rows.

Change to C.

Work 2 rows.

Next row K2tog, k to last 2 sts, k2tog.

Work 3 rows.

Cast off.

With RS facing, k across 18 sts on holder and rep from ** to **.

NECK

With A, cast on 30 sts.

Beg with a k row, work 5 rows.

Next row P2tog, p to last 2 sts, p2tog.

Rep the last 6 rows twice more.

Work 7 rows.

Next row P2tog, p to last 2 sts, p2tog.

Work 15 rows.

Next row P2tog, p to last 2 sts, p2tog. 20 sts.

Work 18 rows.

Cast off.

FRONT OF HEAD (MAKE TWO)

With A, cast on 13 sts.

Beg with a k row, work 10 rows.

Next row K2tog, k to last 2 sts, k2tog.

Work 4 rows.

Dec 1 st at each end of the next 3 rows. 5 sts.

Cast off.

TO MAKE UP

Weave in all yarn ends.

Lay work out flat and press under a damp cloth.

TO EMBROIDER

With B, embroider French knots all over body, legs and neck.

TO FINISH

Stitch legs and under body seams, leaving an opening for the stuffing.

Stuff firmly and sew up opening.

Bend legs to a standing position and stitch them in place to the under body.

Join long neck seam leaving cast-on and cast-off edges open.

Fold in half and stitch across cast-off edge.

Stuff firmly and sew cast-on edge to body with neck seam at front.

Join the two head pieces together around the edge, leaving cast-on edges open, stuff slightly and sew to top of neck.

Eyes – Taking stitches through the head and pulling tightly, sew buttons to each side of head.

Ears – Using the ear template on page 135, cut two pieces of suede. Pinch ear in half lengthways and stitch securely to top of head.

Tail – Using the tail template on page 135, cut a piece of suede approximately 6cm long and 8mm wide.

Cut a fringe at one end, slightly roll and sew firmly into position to end of body.

Tie ribbon around neck and trim ends.

AFTERCARE

Sponge with a wet cloth, hand wash or place in a washing machine at 30°.

NIGHTIE AND HAT

see pages 72–75

A snug and practical piece for small babies, made in fine natural cotton. Knitted in stocking stitch with an envelope neck, integral scratch mittens and an easy access hem with press-studs for a modern take on a classic newborn trousseau

SIZE
To fit newborn(0–3: 3–6) months

MATERIALS
5 x 50g balls of 4ply weight cotton, such as Rowan 4ply Cotton in cream or shale
Pair each size 3mm and 3.25mm knitting needles
15cm of 1.5cm wide cotton tape
4 x 1cm mother of pearl buttons (2 each for nightie and hat)
4 x 2cm mother of pearl buttons for nightie

TENSION
27 sts and 36 rows to 10cm square over st st using 3.25mm needles. Always work a tension swatch and change needles accordingly if necessary.

ABBREVIATIONS
See page 139.

TIPS AND TECHNIQUES
Fully fashioned increase
K3, m1, kto last 3 sts, m1, k3.
Fully fashioned decrease
On a k row:
K3, k2tog, k to last 5 sts, k2tog tbl, k3.
On a p row:
P3, p3tog tbl, p to last 5 sts, p2tog, p3.

NIGHTIE

BACK
Using 3mm needles, cast on 92 (100: 108) sts and beg with a k row, work 11 rows in st st.
Next row (WS) K (to make fold line for hem).
Change to 3.25mm needles and beg with a k row, cont in st st and dec 1 st (see note on fully fashioned decreasing) at each end of 13th and every following 8th row, until 62 (68: 74) sts rem.
Cont straight until work measures 40 (43: 48)cm from fold line, ending with RS facing for next row.
SHAPE ARMHOLES
Cast off 2 sts at beg of next 2 rows. 58 (64: 70) sts.
Dec 1 st, (see note on fully fashioned decreasing) at each end of next row and every foll alt row until 52 (58: 64) sts rem. **
Cont straight until armhole measures 8 (9: 10)cm, ending with WS facing for next row.
SHAPE ENVELOPE NECK
Next row P20 (21: 22) sts, turn and leave rem sts on a holder.
Cast off 3 sts at neck edge on next row and foll 2 alt rows, placing marker at armhole edge of last row. 11 (12: 13) sts.
Dec 1 st at neck edge on every row, at the same time, inc 1 st (see note on fully fashioned increasing) at armhole edge on every foll 3rd row until 4 incs have been worked. 3 (4: 5) sts.
Work 1 row and dec 1 st at neck edge.
Cast off rem 2 (3: 4) sts.
With WS facing, slip centre 12 (16: 20) sts onto a holder, rejoin yarn to rem sts, p to end of row and complete to match first side reversing shaping.

FRONT

Work as Back to **.

Cont straight until armhole measures 4 (5: 6)cm, ending with WS facing for next row.

SHAPE ENVELOPE NECK

Next row P21 (24: 27) sts, turn and leave rem sts on holder.

Dec 1 st (see note on fully fashioned decreasing) at neck edge on every row until 19 (18: 17) sts rem, then on next row and every foll alt row until 11 (12: 13) sts rem. Work 2 rows straight, placing marker at armhole edge of last row.

Dec 1 st at neck edge on every row, at the same time, inc 1 st at armhole edge on every foll 3rd row until 4 incs have been worked. 3 (4: 5) sts.

Work 1 row and dec 1 st at neck edge.

Cast off.

With WS facing, slip centre 10 sts onto a holder, rejoin yarn to rem sts, p to end of row and complete to match first side reversing shaping.

SLEEVES WITH SCRATCH MITTENS

Using 3.25mm needles, cast on 16 sts and work 2 rows in k1, p1 rib.

Beg with a k row, work 13 rows in st st, ending with WS facing for next row.

Change to 3mm needles.

Next 2 rows Cast on 9 (10: 11) sts and work in k1, p1 rib across all sts. 34 (36: 38) sts.

Place a marker at each end of last row.

Change to 3.25mm needles and beg with a k row, work in st st and inc 1 st (see note on fully fashioned increasing) at each end of 5th and every foll 6th row until there are 50 (54: 58) sts.

Cont straight until sleeve measures 15 (17: 19)cm from markers, ending with RS facing for next row.

SHAPE TOP

Cast off 2 sts at beg of next 2 rows. 46 (50: 54) sts.

Dec 1 st at each end of next row and every foll alt row until 34 (38: 42) sts rem.

P 1 row.

Cast off loosely.

FRONT NECKBAND

With RS facing and 3mm needles, pick up and k33 (35: 37) sts along right neck, k across 10 sts from holder, 33 (35: 37) sts up left neck. 76 (80: 84) sts.

Work 3 rows in k1, p1 rib.

Cast off in rib.

BACK NECKBAND

With RS facing and 3mm needles, pick up and knit 24 (25: 26) sts along right neck, 12 (16: 20) sts from holder, 24 (25: 26) sts up left neck. 60 (66: 72) sts.

Work 3 rows in k1, p1 rib.

Cast off in rib.

TO FINISH

Weave in any yarn ends.

Lay work out flat and gently steam.

Place back over front matching markers at armhole edge and catch in place to make envelope neck.

Sew sleeves into armholes, easing to fit.

Fold scratch mitten flap up onto right side of sleeve and tack in place at sides.

Join sleeve seams.

Fold back and front along fold line and slip stitch hem in place.

Join side seams from top of hem to armhole.

Sew large press-stud fasteners to wrong side of hem, evenly spaced, then sew large buttons onto right side of front over press studs.

Cut a small piece of tape, tie in the centre and attach at centre front or sew 2 small buttons to centre front.

HAT

Using 3mm needles, cast on 78 (88: 98) sts and work 4cm in k1, p1 rib, inc 0 (1: 2) sts at centre of last row. 78 (89: 100) sts.

Change to 3.25mm needles and beg with a k row, work in st st until work measures 7.5cm from cast-on edge, ending with RS facing for next row.

Next row K1, [k2tog, k5 (6: 7)] to end of row. 67 (78: 89) sts.

Work 3 rows.

Next row K1, [k2tog, k4 (5: 6)] to end of row. 56 (67: 78) sts.

Work 3 rows.

Next row K1, [k2tog, k3 (4: 5)] to end of row. 45 (56: 67) sts.

Work 3 rows.

Next row K1, [k2tog, k2 (3: 4)] to end of row. 34 (45: 56) sts.

Work 1 (3: 3) rows.

Next row K1, [k2tog, k1 (2: 3)] to end of row. 23 (34: 45) sts.

Work 1 (1: 3) rows.

2ND AND 3RD SIZES ONLY

Next row K1, [k2tog, k– (1: 2)] to end of row. – (23: 34) sts.

Work 1 row.

3RD SIZE ONLY

Next row K1, [k2tog, k– (–: 1)] to end of row. – (–: 23) sts.

Work 1 row.

ALL SIZES

Next row K1, [k2tog] to end of row. 12 sts.

Work 1 row.

Next row [K2tog] to end of row. 6 sts.

Thread yarn through rem sts, pull up tightly and fasten off.

TO FINISH

Weave in any yarn ends.

Lay work out flat and gently steam.

Join seam.

Cut a small piece of tape, fold in half and attach towards one side of hat, or sew 2 small buttons towards one side of hat.

TEMPLATES

TEDDY BEAR
see pages 80–83

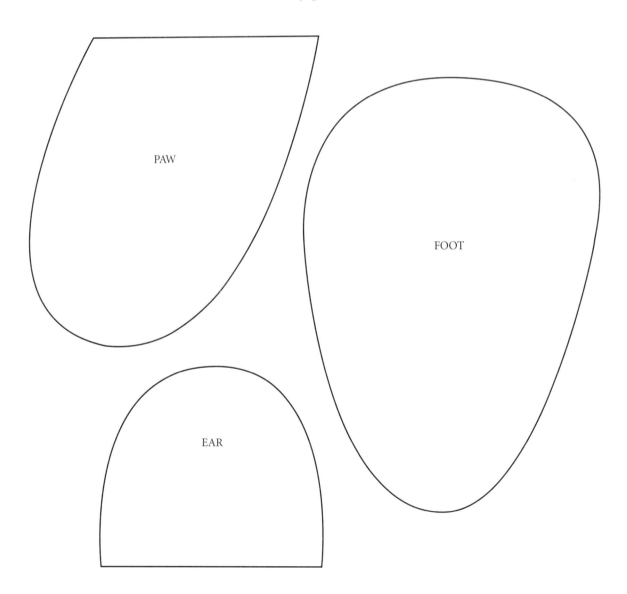

PAW

FOOT

EAR

BIRD MOBILE
see pages 120–121

SPOTTY GIRAFFE
see pages 128–129

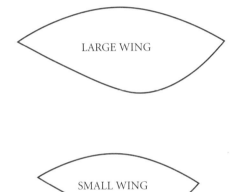

LARGE WING

SMALL WING

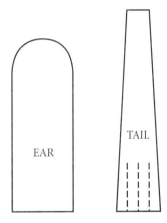

EAR

TAIL

RECOMMENDED YARNS

The following is a list of the yarns used in this book. Although I have recommended a specific yarn for each project, you can use substitutes if you prefer. If you decide to use an alternative, purchase a substitute that is as close as possible to the original yarn in thickness, weight and texture so it will work with the pattern instructions. Buy only one ball to start with, so you can test the effect. Calculate the number of balls you need by meterage rather than weight. The recommended knitting-needle size and tension on the ball bands are extra guides to the yarn thickness. To obtain Lanaknits, R.E. Dickie British Breeds, Rowan And Yeoman's yarns, go to the websites below to find a mail-order stockist or store in your area:

www.lanaknits.com / www.hempforknitting.com
www.britishwool.com
www.knitrowan.com
www.ryclassic.com
www.yeomansyarns.com

LANAKNITS ALLHEMP6 DK
A double-knitting-weight hemp yarn
Recommended knitting-needle size: 3.75mm
Tension: 22 sts x 28 rows per 10cm over knitted st st
Skein size: 150m per 100g skein
Yarn specification: 100% hemp

LANAKNITS CASHMERE CANAPA DK
A double-knitting-weight cotton-blend yarn
Recommended knitting-needle size: 3.75mm
Tension: 22 sts x 34 rows per 10cm over knitted st st
Skein size: 110m per 50g ball
Yarn specification: 60% cotton, 30% cashmere, 10% hemp

R.E. DICKIE BRITISH BREEDS ARAN NATURAL
An aran-weight wool yarn
Recommended knitting-needle size: 5mm
Tension: 18 sts per 10cm over knitted st st
Ball size: 120m per 100g ball
Yarn specification: 100% wool

ROWAN CLASSIC (RYC) BABY ALPACA DK
A double-knitting-weight wool yarn
Recommended knitting-needle size: 4mm
Tension: 22 sts x 30 rows per 10cm over knitted st st
Ball size: 100m per 50g ball
Yarn specification: 100% baby alpaca

ROWAN CLASSIC (RYC) BAMBOO SOFT DK
A double-knitting-weight bamboo yarn
Recommended knitting-needle size: 3.75mm
Tension: 25 sts x 30 rows per 10cm over knitted st st
Ball size: 102m per 50g ball
Yarn specification: 100% bamboo

ROWAN FINE MILK COTTON 4PLY
A fine-weight 4ply cotton-blend yarn
Recommended knitting-needle size: 2.75mm
Tension: 30 sts x 38 rows per 10cm over knitted st st
Ball size: 150m per 50g ball
Yarn specification: 70% cotton, 30% milk protein

ROWAN PURELIFE ORGANIC COTTON NATURALLY DYED DK
A double-knitting-weight organic cotton yarn
Recommended knitting-needle size: 3.75mm
Tension: 22 sts x 30 rows per 10cm over knitted st st
Ball size: 120m per 50g ball
Yarn specification: 100% organic cotton

ROWAN PURELIFE BRITISH SHEEPS BREED UNDYED
An aran-weight pure wool yarn
Recommended knitting-needle size: 7mm
Tension: 13 sts x 18 rows per 10cm over knitted st st
Ball size: 110m per 100g ball
Yarn specification: 100% wool

YEOMAN'S COTTON CANNELE 4PLY
A fine-weight 4ply mercerized cotton yarn
Recommended knitting-needle size: 2.75mm
Tension: 33 sts x 44 rows per 10cm over knitted st st
Cone size: 850m per 250g cone
Yarn specification: 100% cotton

PATTERN INSTRUCTIONS

Each garment is given in three different sizes ranging from 0–3 months to 9–12 months. The smallest size is given first and appears outside the round ( ) brackets. The larger sizes are given inside the brackets in ascending order. When working through the instructions, your size will be in the same position throughout the pattern. If only one number is given, it applies to all three of the sizes and where 0 appears no stitches or rows are worked for this size. To avoid any confusion, highlight the relevant instructions for your size within the pattern. Where instructions are given in square [ ] brackets or between * asterisks, work these instructions the number of time stated after the brackets or asterisk.

ABBREVIATIONS

All knitting patterns follow a basic structure and use the same standard abbreviations and terminology.

alt	alternate
approx	approximately
beg	begin(ning)
cm	centimetre(s)
cont	continu(e)(ing)
dec	decreas(e)(ing)
foll	follow(s)(ing)
g	gramme(s)
garter st	garter stitch (k every row)
in	inch(es)
inc	increas(e)(ing)
k	knit
LH	left hand
m	metre(s)
m1	make one stitch by picking up horizontal loop before next stitch and working into back of it
mm	millimetre(s)
p	purl
patt	pattern
psso	pass slipped stitch over
rem	remain(s)(ing)
rep	repeat(ing)
rev st st	reverse stocking stitch (p all RS rows, k all WS rows)
RH	right hand
RS	right side
skpo	slip 1, knit 1, pass slipped stitch over (one stitch decreased)
sl	slip
st(s)	stitch(es)
st st	stocking stitch (k all RS rows, p all WS rows)
tbl	through back of loop(s)
tog	together
WS	wrong side
yfwd	yarn forward and over right needle to make a new stitch
yon	yarn over right needle to make a new stitch

GARMENT CARE

When you invest so much time in creating a hand-knitted garment, great care should be taken in the laundering of these items. How frequent a garment needs washing depends on how it is worn, but childrenswear often needs laundering on a regular basis. The yarn you use must be able to stand up to this, but this does not necessarily mean that all yarns must be machine washable. Look at the labels: those on most commercial yarns have instructions for washing or dry cleaning, drying and pressing. So, for a project knitted in one yarn only, a quick look at the yarn label will tell you how to care for it. If you wish to work with several yarns in one piece of work, the aftercare requires a little more thought. If one label suggests dry cleaning, then be sure to dry clean the garment.

WASHING

If in doubt about whether or not your knitting is washable, then make a little swatch of the yarns. Wash this to see if the fabric is affected by being immersed in water or not, watching for shrinkage and stretching. If you are satisfied with the results, go ahead and wash the knitting by hand in lukewarm water. Never use hot water, as this will 'felt' your fabric, and you will not be able to return it to its pre-washed state. In particular, wool tends to react to major changes in temperature.

When washing any knitted item, handle it carefully. There should be enough water to cover the garment completely and the soap should be thoroughly dissolved before immersing it. If you need to sterilise any garment that has become badly soiled or stained, then use a proprietary brand of steriliser for this purpose. As a precaution, test wash any trims you use before you make up the garment with them. Nothing is more infuriating than to spoil an entire garment because the trim colours run in the wash. Natural fibres such as wool, cotton and silk are usually better washed by hand, and in pure soap, than in a machine. However, should you decide to wash any knitted garment in a washing machine, place it inside a pillowslip as an extra precaution. Soap flakes are kinder to sensitive skins than most detergents, provided all traces of the soap are removed in the rinsing process.

RINSING

Squeeze out any excess water, never wring it out. Rinse thoroughly, until every trace of soap is removed, as any left in will mat the fibres and may irritate the skin. Use at least two changes of water or continue until the water is clear and without soap bubbles. Take care, too, to keep the rinsing water the same temperature as the washing water.

SPINNING

The garments can be rinsed on a short rinse and spin as part of the normal washing machine programme for delicate fabrics. Again, as an extra precaution, place the item to be spun inside a pillowslip.

DRYING

Squeeze the garment between towels or fold in a towel and gently spin. Do not hang wet knitting up to dry, as the weight of the water will stretch it out of shape. To dry, lay the knitting out flat on top of a towel, which will absorb some of the moisture. Ease the garment into shape. Dry away from direct heat and leave flat until completely dry.

PRESSING

When the garment is dry, ease it into shape. Check the yarn label before pressing your knitting as most fibres only require a little steam, and the iron should be applied gently. Alternatively, press with a damp cloth between the garment and the iron.

REMOVING STAINS

Stains are a fact of life. The best solution with any stain is to remove the garment while the stain is still wet and soak it thoroughly in cold, never hot, water. Failing that, use a proprietary stain remover.

ACKNOWLEDGEMENTS

For me, the unique joy of creating knitwear for babies and the pleasure derived from using natural, sustainable yarns go hand in hand. And they are both topics within craft that I am passionate about. What has made this book extra special is the team who have shared my passion throughout and at the same time made invaluable contributions of their own.

I have long admired the sublime photography of KRISTIN PERERS, with its understated, often painterly qualities, and wanted no one else for this particular project. Working with ALEX LEWIS, who brought his distinctive styling (as well as his own childhood baby clothes) to the shoots, together their emotive images have made this more than a knitting book. My heartfelt thanks.

The exceptional team at Quadrille Publishing, ALISON CATHIE's exemplary company. A publisher of exacting style and vision who continually exceed the boundaries. JANE O'SHEA, my editorial director and mentor, whose innate ability to question and encourage with style and vision is exacting and accurate always. My sincere appreciation and thanks to creative director HELEN LEWIS and designer CLAIRE PETERS for their inherent understanding, ingenious innovation and meticulous detail in realising the vision. This book would simply not have happened without LISA PENDREIGH, my project editor, her professionalism and patience is without equal, and her passion and support, both aesthetic and pragmatic is unrivalled. And I am indebted as always to ROSY TUCKER for her painstaking hard work in checking all the patterns – invaluable and reassuring.

Huge appreciation and thanks for the contribution made by SALLY LEE, my creative practitioner for her unswerving support, enthusiasm, expertise and friendship. Also to CHRISTINE DILLEY and MARY POTTER for their superb hand-knitting skills. Special thanks to EILEEN BUNDY for her unique creativity and expertise, dispensed with encouraging cups of coffee.

To ROWAN, Lana Hames of LANAKNITS and Tony Brook of YEOMAN YARNS thanks for, first of all, creating yarns of the highest quality and innovation, but invaluably for their generosity in contributing yarns and enthusiastic support for this book.

Finally to my daughter, ARABELLA, for tireless practical and emotional support and IAN, for keeping it focused and coherent. Thank you both.

PUBLISHER'S ACKNOWLEDGEMENTS

The publisher would like to thank the following for loaning clothes, accessories and other items: Angelique (angelique.co.uk), Baileys Home and Garden (baileyshomeandgarden.com), Caravan (caravanstyle.com), Farm Yarn Natural Alpaca Wool (farmyarn.co.uk), Kitchen Garden Antiques (pearjo@msn.com), The Cloth Shop (clothshop.net), Vintage Heaven (vintageheaven.co.uk).

Editorial director Jane O'Shea
Creative director Helen Lewis
Project editor Lisa Pendreigh
Designer Claire Peters
Photographer Kristin Perers
Stylist Alex Lewis
Pattern checker Rosy Tucker
Illustrator Bridget Bodoano
Production director Vincent Smith
Production controller Ruth Deary

First published in 2009 by
Quadrille Publishing Ltd
Alhambra House
27–31 Charing Cross Road
London WC2H 0LS
www.quadrille.co.uk

Text and project designs
© 2009 Erika Knight
Photography
© 2009 Kristin Perers
Artwork, design and layout
© 2009 Quadrille Publishing Ltd

British Library Cataloguing-in-Publication Data
A catalogue record for this book is available from the British Library.

ISBN: 978 184400 707 3

Printed in Singapore